LIES
that Destroy
HOPE

By
Gary Paul Maltman

LIES
that Destroy
HOPE

Gary Paul Maltman

MEGA
CORPORATION

ISBN: 1–890436–05–4

Printed in the United States of America

Contents

Acknowledgments

I would like to acknowledge the help and support of my wife, Theresa, and our four children — Shalis, Ricky, Zachery, and Caleb.

I would also like to acknowledge the members and friends we have at our church home, Lakewood Baptist.

• • • • • •

Special appreciation is extended to Dr. T.B. Boyd III and the staff for making this work possible.

• • • • • •

Finally, I would like to acknowledge those whose lives are limited or hurting because they have been deceived by Satan's lies. Christians and nonbelievers alike must recognize how Satan uses lies to cause devastation in their lives.

Through reading this book, it is my hope that they will recognize that truth, revealed to us through our Savior, Jesus Christ, is the antidote for lies and the restorer of hope.

About the Author

G ary Paul Maltman is a missionary committed to spreading the truths of the Gospel of Jesus Christ. He and his wife, Theresa, have both served as missionaries in Bolivia.

In a previous work entitled *Christians in Spiritual Warfare* (Boyd Publications, 1998), Maltman demonstrated that Christians are in a war with opposing spiritual forces. Christians must use the weaponry that God has given us to fight Satan.

Maltman was motivated to write the book because he believes there are many people who are not where God would have them to be spiritually. Through personal experience and observation, Maltman was inspired to create this work.

Maltman graduated from the University of Texas at Arlington with a bachelor's degree in communications. He has been employed as a senior copywriter for a major advertising agency where he wrote advertising copy for a number of major corporations, including Fortune 500® companies.

Maltman lives in Lavergne, Tennessee with his wife and their four children. They are members of Lakewood Baptist Church in Donelson.

Lie #1:
"My Situation Is Hopeless!"

Let's be very frank. Probably the greatest lie used by Satan to destroy the lives and futures of individuals, churches, organizations, cities, states, countries, and even the world is to have them believe in the illusion of hopelessness. The belief that there is no hope is one of the most powerful tools created by Satan to make an individual contribute to his or her own demise. If Satan can take away your hope, he can even rob you of your faith in the truths of the Bible and God.

You may believe that nothing can take away your faith in God and His Son, Jesus, and God's Holy Spirit. But if you say "There is no hope," or believe that there is no hope, you are denying the very existence of God and His Son Jesus Christ and God's Holy Spirit! By accepting and acting upon the claim of hopelessness, you are saying through your actions, "There is no hope, even in God. There is no hope, even in Jesus Christ."

You are saying, "There is no hope in what the Bible teaches. There is no hope in prayer. God is not in control. Even He cannot help."

Have you ever found yourself living according to this belief? If you have, you have been sold one of the greatest untruths ever used against humankind. Just as God loves you, Satan despises you equally so. He hates you even more than your worst enemy! Satan wants you to accept hopelessness as your reality so that you won't attempt to see the hope that surrounds you by Christ Jesus.

Yes, it's true! Hope is all around you! No matter what your current predicament is—no matter what your physical condition is, no matter what your educational level is, regardless if you have a criminal record, no matter what your financial situation looks like, no matter what your spiritual condition looks like right now, no matter what tragedy you are experiencing—there is hope for you!

Did you know there is potentially as much hope around you on the worst day of your life as there is on the most glorious day of your life? The difference lies in your focus!

Where do you place your trust? If your trust lies in only what you can see, hear, smell, or taste, you are destined for a hopeless existence. Satan tricks us into using our own understanding to determine the outcome of a situation. He will use us against ourselves to destroy ourselves, if we allow him. Satan uses human understanding to rob each of us of personal hope.

What other method could more effectively be used to bring successful businessmen and businesswomen, movie stars, music stars, sports stars, even millionaires and other seemingly successful people to the point of suicide?

If you are feeling that you are without hope right now, it would be ludicrous to suggest things have not gone awry in your life. But your current circumstance is not the real issue. The point is that the biggest way the tragedy you have experienced can be used to rob hope from you is if you allow the situation to change your focus.

Tragedy, shock, disbelief, or severe disappointment often, by the very nature of your surviving them, change your focus. Unfortunately, the main things that get out of focus are the areas wherein lies that greatest potential for hope in your life.

Satan uses the negatives of a situation to bring you down. When you experience tragedy, there indeed may be tons of negatives to consider. That point not being argued, you cannot allow those negative actions to distract you from the hope God provides, even in the midst of tragedy. The reality is God-given hope for your life. The key, however, is that you likely will have to work hard to remove your focus from the negatives.

What does your heart most desire? Wealth? Fame? Love? Health? Youth? Perhaps you want a chance to start over.

Only you know what you think will bring you happiness. But think about it—what is it about that item or condition that you think would bring you happiness? As you consider what it would take to bring you happiness, remember that nothing or no one outside of yourself can bring you happiness.

Regardless of what you place inside the void that stands between you and happiness, you must recognize that the peace you desire comes from the hope you place in that condition. But that does not necessarily mean that you will gain peace and happiness once you have acquired what you sought.

If you knew that nothing would change today, but that in one week you would have exactly what you want, would you feel better today? Of course you would! Although you would not yet have the item or condition, you would have peace in the hope that life will get better.

If you were assured that your desire was forthcoming, you would not focus on what you can see today. Instead, your focus would be on the assurance that there is hope in your future.

You can do it right now! Start changing your focus this very minute. One day at a time, one hour at a time, one minute at a time, you can change your focus from hopelessness to hope; but it starts right now.

Begin to focus on this question: What if God does have a way for me to have true hope? The question has already been answered. God does!

What if you could find hope in the Bible or through daily prayer? You can, if you begin to focus on God and His will for your life instead of the things you think it would take to make you happy! God wants what is best for your life—trust Him.

When someone wants the best for you, that's hope! Study the Bible and pray daily. There is hope through Jesus Christ!

Bible Verses to Overcome Lie #1

- "Happy is he that hath the God of Jacob for his help, whose hope is in the Lord his God." Psalm 146:5 (KJV)

- "But if we hope for that we see not, then do we with patience wait for it." Romans 8:25 (KJV)

Related Scripture Passages

- Luke 1:5-23
- Romans 10:1-13
- 2 Corinthians 4
- 1 Samuel 17

Suggested Prayer Focus

1. Ask God to reveal to you the real reason(s) you believe that there is no hope for you.

2. Ask God to show you what you can do to change or remove those reasons for lost hope.

3. Pray for the Holy Spirit to help you distinguish between the things you can change and the ones you can't.

4. Pray for God to help you change your focus from the negatives in your life to His will for your life.

5. Pray for God to lead you to through His Word which will help to restore your hope.

6. Pray for inner peace and hope, regardless of your present circumstances.

7. Repent and pray for strength to stay on the right course.

8. Thank and praise God for all things. Realizing what God has done and is doing for you will help you to know that He can do even more.

9. Pray that God will give you a heart to be more concerned about others feeling a sense of hopelessness than about your own circumstances.

Steps to Take to Overcome Lie #1

1. When thoughts about things you cannot change start to get you down, surrender those thoughts to God immediately! You can praise God for good thoughts to change issues in your life.

2. Make a list of the things you need God's help to change about yourself and your life. Rank them in order, from the easiest to change to the most difficult.

3. Every day, attempt to do something—anything and everything you can—to make the changes for the better.

4. Update your "changes desired and steps toward change" list as changes are made.

5. On a separate sheet of paper, write down realistic expectations of what you would like your life to be like: (1) in one year; (2) in five years; and (3) in ten years.

6. On that second sheet of paper, make a list of things you should do to accomplish those goals.

7. On that same page, make another list of things that may hinder achieving those goals.

8. Commit those lists to memory and pray for the strength and wisdom to accomplish all your future decisions with the help of the Lord.

9. Ask a compassionate, trusted Christian counselor or friend to review your list for realistic expectations and scriptural alignment.

10. Study stories of other believers in the Bible who were once in similar circumstances, then work diligently to overcome those circumstances through the Lord.

11. Read, the stories over and over so you will not begin to lose hope.

12. Avoid or minimize contact with negative people, conversations, and thoughts. Increase your contact with positive people, conversations, and thoughts.

Lie #2: "All of My Options Are Negative!"

This could be called the "near-sighted" lie. This lie assumes that only the options you can think of at this moment are the only choices you have. This is the lie that feeds off of an unwillingness to search for, create, or work toward better choices. Maybe it's only your most obvious choices that are the bad ones.

Many times, because of the intensity of the "situations" we find ourselves in, we are very short sighted in evaluating our options and long-term results. Often it is because we accept the suggestion that there are only two choices in every situation—yes or no, now or never, accept or reject. The choices are not always only "Yes" or "No."

Sometimes the choices are not only "Yes" or "No," but "Yes, with this stipulation or change," or "No, not now, but maybe later."

"Now or never" may really be "now or at a different time." Likewise, the choice of "accept or reject" can develop into "improve or reject."

Even a computer, that ultimately reads every bit of information as a choice between "zero" or "one," will go on to the next step after every choice. As long as it continues to move forward in its processes, the choices and answers can change in an "If this, then this..." scenario.

You are in the same situation. Even if the only choices you can envision currently are bad, then what? Think and pray some more. What good choices would be available next? Move forward in your thinking process and don't give up hope with the very first answer!

Is there any way possible that one of your first options could lead to better choices? If so, even your worst first option eventually has good choices that follow. But first stop and seek godly input!

Why do you think that all of your options are negative? Is that really true, or did you come to this conclusion without godly counsel? Is there any way possible that any of the choices can be replaced by a better choice? Have you prayed to God for direction or insight?

If your best friends were in this situation instead of you, and they were panicked because they thought they had only bad choices, what suggestions would you offer to them? Can you make those same suggestions to yourself?

The best way to find out if the "All of my options are negative" lie applies to you is to ask yourself as many questions as possible. First, what do you believe are your choices? Then ask yourself why you are limited to those choices. Pray and think carefully. Ask yourself if you have really examined all of your options. Seek out someone with whom you can discuss what you believe your real choices are in your situation.

Do you need a confidant to provide you insight into additional choices if the first appears to be all bad? Are all of your options actually as bad as they appear, or are you simply resisting change?

Take time and consider the results of each of the options before you. Think about whether it is really necessary to choose right away. When considering each possibility, think about any additional rights, responsibilities, or choices available to you in your current situation.

In reality, some of the most helpful questions, as well as their answers, come from the Bible. What guidance does the Bible give in this situation? What would a wise person choose to do, in accordance with the teachings of the Book of Proverbs? What would Jesus do? What hope does the Bible promise that will lead you to consider, create, or enhance new good choices?

There are more questions you can ask yourself, but if you stop right now and ask yourself these questions and answer them, you will begin to see hope. Answer them with whatever knowledge you currently have; read the Bible for guidance; pray for answers and immediately seek godly counsel from Christian leaders whom you can trust. You will know if there are any good or better choices!

Bible Verses to Overcome Lie #2

- "Hear counsel, and receive instruction, that thou mayest be wise in the latter end." Proverb 19:20 (KJV)

- "Without counsel, purposes are disappointed: but in the multitude of counsellors they are established." Proverb 15:22 (KJV)

Related Scripture Passages

- Daniel 6
- Matthew 25:14-30
- Proverbs 2
- Proverbs 3

Suggested Prayer Focus

1. Pray for God to give you peace as you consider your options and discern the right choices.

2. Pray for wisdom as you make your choices.

3. Ask God to reveal any and all choices He will have you consider.

4. Ask God to direct you to the specific choice or choices that are in keeping with His will.

5. Pray that you will not to be distracted or hasty while making a decision.

6. Pray for the Holy Spirit to call to your mind Bible verses that will help you choose wisely.

7. Ask God to block Satan and his demonic activity from the decision process.

8. Ask God to touch and prepare the hearts of those who make decisions that affect your choices.

9. Pray for God's will to be done in your life, above your own desires and all else.

10. Pray for peace if God's will does not include the option you desire.

11. Pray that those who may be affected by your choices, and those who may judge your choices will have compassion and understanding.

Steps to Take to Overcome Lie #2

1. Write down your specific goal in the situation that is troubling you now. If you can determine your deadline for making a decision, write that down as well.

2. Whatever the amount of time remaining until the deadline (whether it is minutes, hours, days, weeks, or years), cut that time in half and make it a goal to have made your "trial choice" by that time.

3. Make a list of all the options you believe are open to you at this point in time.

4. From that list, write down each choice on its own piece or side of paper. For each choice, make a "pros" column and a "cons" column to list and compare the aspects of each choice.

5. When you have done that for each choice, find the sheet with the greatest number of good choices and the least number of bad choices. This should start to lead you in the direction of the right choice. If there are several sheets with an equal number of good and bad choices, you might have several options that would be equally good.

6. Avoid making a sudden decision that "This is it," based on fear or panic.

7. Continue listing both positive and negative points of each choice until the time for the "trial choice" must be made (half the time until the real choice must be made–see #2).

8. Take each choice to the next "step" as if you had chosen that one and continue to compare positive versus negative points until you are satisfied you have made the best "trial" choice.

9. At the appointed time for the "trial choice," make your final choice.

10. Take your results (time permitting) to a trusted advisor who you know makes wise godly decisions. Discuss your choice with that person. Compare your choice to what Scripture teaches you to do. Research additional input. Keep in mind, however, that the ultimate Advisor is the Holy Spirit. More than human opinion, depend on the guidance of the Holy Spirit to lead you to the right choice.

11. Set a new "trial" choice time that is halfway between the time when you make that first choice and deadline for the real choice.

12. Repeat this process, as allowed, until you have prayerfully made the best choice.

Lie #3: *"I Don't Have a Choice!"*

A popular secular rock song from the 1980's states, "If you choose not to decide, you still have made a choice." Though the messenger may not be ideal in this case, the message still holds true.

Even in the bleakest of situations, there is always a choice. This does not mean you will always be able to choose the outcome of a given situation. It means that you will always have a choice in how you are going to react!

Does this apply to your life on a daily, weekly, monthly, yearly, or even permanent basis? Yes, it applies to every situation you have ever faced in your life. More importantly, it applies to every situation you ever will experience or endure while you are on this earth.

What is your situation and why do you feel that you have no choice? Are you saying, "Well for starters, I didn't ask to be born"? If you're thinking that way, you are absolutely right. You didn't ask to be born. But you were born. Now what? You are here. Since God deemed it necessary for you to be born, and God never makes mistakes, you must determine how to get through life the best way possible.

Your birthday is your first lesson in reality concerning choices in your life. Your birth was not a choice you made. Regardless of your circumstances, how you live is a choice you can optimize depending on your decisions for your life. God gave you life, but you must choose what the quality of your life will be.

Whether you have made a decision to give your life to Jesus Christ, or whether you have decided to reject Jesus and His teachings, your life is full of choices! However, those choices will be greatly affected by whether your life is guided by Christ or guided by self.

Were you born into a situation that was not your personal preference? How can you change that today? Can you undo it? The answer is a resounding "No!" The real question is "Can you overcome it?" The answer is an unqualified "Yes, you can!"

Do you believe that you have no choice in your present situation? Is there anything you can do to extricate yourself from it? You have some choices. (They may not be your "ideal" choices, but every choice you face in life will not be an "ideal" or perfect choice.) As imperfect as your options may seem, remember that in every situation, you do have a choice!

You may ask, "What happens when someone is robbed, raped, molested, fired, injured, sued, imprisoned, or even audited by the Internal Revenue Service?"

What choices did the Jews have when they were arrested, tortured and placed in gas chambers by the Nazis? What choices did the black people who were enslaved in this country have? What choices did and do persecuted Christians have?"

These were all bad and ungodly situations and are not to be taken lightly and forgotten. When someone is robbed, he or she can choose to cooperate with the robber and reduce chances of injury or death. The person being robbed can choose to watch for an opportunity to overcome the robber. After the robbery, the person can choose to report it, testify, overcome the ordeal and move on, or not.

A person who has been raped has the choice of giving up on life or seeking professional help and God's love, faith and determination to begin life again in a hard, painful and long process.

A person who is fired, injured, or sued has choices as to whether he or she will react emotionally and vengefully or logically and positively. An injured person can if possible undergo any and every available rehabilitation procedure to improve his or her quality of life.

Those who are imprisoned can do the best they can, choose to make their period of confinement profitable or make things worse by not turning to God for help, hope, and comfort.

Author Viktor E. Frankl has shared how he learned about choices from his experience in a Nazi concentration camp. He learned that the last, and ultimate, freedom any human being has is power to choose one's attitude toward any given situation.

Countless numbers of blacks who were enslaved in this country had to make a choice. They knew that although their bodies were in bondage, their spirits could not be. The Jews in the concentration camps, slaves, and history's persecuted Christians, in more deplorable situations than you and I will ever face, had some choices. They could choose, even in their nakedness, starvation, bondage, and torture, to accept the hope of salvation and a perfect eternity through the God of Jesus Christ. They could pass God's hope to their children, or they could choose to teach their children and others around them to hate those who tortured and killed their friends and families. These oppressed people did not hate God, they did not understand the "whys" of their horrible situation

They could choose to close their eyes and pray to God for mercy and strength, or they could use what little strength they had left to lift their fists to God and curse Him for the atrocities evil persons had dealt them.

If you are raising your fist to God right now and cursing Him, along with those who have harmed you and your family, it is a choice you are making this very moment. If you choose instead to turn from your pain and sadness and give Jesus Christ control of your life, you will have more hope than you ever imagined. You will have the hope of eternity in heaven and help on earth! What a choice!

Bible Verses to Overcome Lie #3

- "And if it seem evil unto you to serve the Lord, choose you this day whom ye will serve..." Joshua 24:15 (KJV)

- "Choosing rather to suffer affliction with the people of God, than to enjoy the pleasures of sin for a season." Hebrews 11:25 (KJV)

Related Scripture Passages

- The Book of Jonah
- Acts 12:1-19
- Proverbs 12
- Romans

Suggested Prayer Focus

1. Ask God to forgive you for any anger or hatred you have directed at those who have harmed you.

2. Pray to feel the love of God and the closeness of Jesus.

3. Ask God for more faith and hope.

4. Pray for strength, and courage.

5. Pray for understanding.

6. Confess to God that His ways are beyond your understanding and pray for more trust in God when you don't understand.

7. Thank and praise God for whatever good that will come from your desperate circumstances.

8. Ask God to use your suffering to bless others who might have to face the same hardship.

9. Pray for the ability to forgive others so you will have a good relationship with the Lord.

Steps to Take to Overcome Lie #3

1. Without dwelling negatively on the past, make a list, recalling every choice you have ever made in life. (This should be a really long list. Do not stop until you finally believe in your heart you have had more choices in your life than you realized.)

2. Reflect on your life and your list. Ask yourself if those choices have reflected the will of God or your own will. Decide whether you will truly serve God or not. Whether you admit it or not, today and every day for the rest of your life, you make a conscious choice to serve or deny God.

3. Choose whether or not you will repent of your sins. Be prepared to accept the consequences of your choice.

4. Choose between blaming God unjustly or Satan rightfully for the evil that has happened to you.

5. Choose between wisely praying for help or just wallowing in the mire of self-pity.

6. Choose between wisely turning to Jesus as your Friend and Savior, or just turning your back on Jesus as Satan would have you do. Think about the consequences of both choices.

7. Choose between wisely asking God for help or just attempting to recover on your own.

8. Choose between wisely admitting your own weaknesses before God or just relying on your own strength.

9. Choose between wisely surrounding yourself with thoughts and conversations about God's greatness or just surrounding yourself with angry thoughts and conversations against life.

10. Choose between wisely seeking God's help by reading the Bible today or just putting it off until later.

11. Choose between wisely filling your mind with godly thoughts about your situation or just filling your mind with worldly thoughts about how to respond to your situation.

12. Choose between wisely addressing the problems facing you or just ignoring them, hoping they will "go away with time." Remember that by not choosing to deal with a problem, you are still making a choice.

13. Choose between wisely and diligently seeking choices with God's help or just believing you have no choices.

Lie #4: "Nobody Has this Problem but Me!"

This lie usually affects us after we have begun to believe one of the other hope-destroying lies of Satan! This lie needs to be addressed, however, because it is a separate lie your conscience may tell you. It may even be something others have led you to believe. This message is probably conveyed to you even through the reality of commercial messages. The key point, again, is that this negative message is simply not true!

What you need to recognize first, however, is the improbability that out of everyone in the world, you are the only one in your situation! Actually, with the billions of people in this world, the statistical chance of your being just like thousands of other people is extremely probable. So what does that mean?

It means that you should not concentrate on the thought that "I'm the only one in my shoes." Think about this—if thousands of people have been in your same situation throughout history, and probably thousands are in the same situation now, there must be some solutions available that someone has already discovered.

You know the old saying, "We're all human"? Well, it's true. As a matter of fact, it's biblical. The Bible says that we all sin and fall short of the glory of God. By God's own design of humankind, He deemed it appropriate and wise to allow humans, all humans, to make mistakes and endure hardships — some we have caused ourselves and some that may not have been created by our own actions.

Thinking you are the only one in your situation basically comes because your focus has been so fine tuned to yourself that you are missing the big picture. This is not healthy for you.

Perhaps you are bed-ridden, or incarcerated, or seemingly alone in a small dorm room on a giant college campus somewhere. Maybe you work as one person among hundreds on an assembly line or in an office. You might live in the city or the country, with or without a family. Your exact circumstance doesn't matter. If you're feeling that you are without hope it's probable that your focus has eliminated everything but yourself and your problem, leading you to feel sorry for yourself.

The Bible says in Matthew 5:45 that our Father in heaven sends "rain on the just and the unjust." This means that everyone is subject to some good times in life and some hard times. That means you can't be the only one in your situation!

The apostle Paul was in prison more times than all the other apostles. He was beaten beyond measure, endured perils on the waters, troubles from his countrymen and from the heathen, in the wilderness and in the cities. Paul was beaten with rods, stoned, shipwrecked, hungry, thirsty, cold, and naked.

Our Lord and Savior Jesus Christ was mocked, lied on, chased out of town, spit on, whipped, hit in the head, had a crown of thorns crammed into His flesh, had nails driven into His hands and feet, and was hung until death on the cross.

Even if it were possible for you to be the only one in your situation, what difference would that make in your commitment to overcome it? Why should that lead you to believe that there are no options for you?

Will you say to yourself, "I am only going to try to overcome this problem if I'm not the only one in the world in this situation?"

Will you say to yourself, "If I'm the only one this ever happened to, I'm just going to concentrate on that and never try to do anything to overcome or endure it?"

It really doesn't help you to dwell on the fact that you believe you are the only to ever face your situation—even if it's true; and it's not!

It is really not as significant whether you are the first person this ever happened to or the ten-millionth; rather, it is how you approach overcoming the situation. Someone who has experienced similar circumstances might actually be able to help you find existing information that will enable you to regain hope.

Whether you are the first or the ten-millionth person to experience your situation, you still must be willing to consider your options for dealing with the situation properly and prayerfully.

While you are dealing with your dilemma, don't concentrate on, "Poor me." Instead, concentrate on finding a godly solution and seeking His grace and comfort until that solution is manifested. The grace and comfort will come through God, through prayer and through reading the Bible. You may also find comfort in talking to Christian counselors, to your pastor, or to biblically grounded Christian friends. Regardless of whom you talk with or what you do, the solution will come from God, even though you might not recognize it as such at the time.

Bible Verses to Overcome Lie #4

- "The thing that hath been, is that which shall be; and that which is done is that which shall be done: and there is no new thing under the sun." Ecclesiastes 1:8 (KJV)

- "And he said unto me, My grace is sufficient for thee: my strength is made perfect in weakness." 2 Corinthians 12:9 (KJV)

Related Scripture Passages

- Numbers 12:1-16
- Matthew 2:16-18
- The Book of Job
- Genesis 39

Suggested Prayer Focus

1. Ask God for release from your pain, suffering, and heartache, if it is in His will.

2. Ask God to change your focus from yourself to Jesus and His will for your life.

3. Pray for God to place people in your path who will be compassionate and understanding.

4. Pray for God to guide you to places where you will receive help and hope.

5. Ask God to reveal passages of Scripture that will deal with your needs specifically and offer you consolation and hope through His promises.

6. Ask God to open your eyes to those who are less fortunate than you so that you will not feel sorry for yourself. Ask Him to show you ways that you can help the less fortunate, even as you struggle through your own situation.

7. Ask God to reveal how your situation might even be used to bring Him glory.

8. Praise Jesus for the suffering, the additional pain, and the cruel death we would also deserve if He had not taken our place.

Steps to Take to Overcome Lie #4

1. If you are sick, but not in a hospital, spend your time praying for those who are in a hospital.

2. If you have physical pain, but still can function somewhat, spend your time praying for those who cannot perform daily functions at all. If possible, get out of the house and do something to help someone else.

3. If you have a broken limb, pray for those who have only one such limb.

4. If you are missing a limb, pray for those who have no limbs.

5. If you are in a wheelchair, pray for those who cannot even get out of bed to get into a wheelchair. Pray also for those who cannot afford to buy a wheelchair.

6. If you have been told that you have only six months to live, pray for others.

7. If you have lost a loved one recently, pray for those who have lost their families recently or those who have never had a loving relationship with their families.

8. If you've lost your whole family recently, pray for those who never knew their family members before they died.

9. If you are hungry or thirsty, pray for those who have already passed out from hunger or thirst and are dying.

10. If you've lost your job recently, pray for those who lost their jobs last year and are still unemployed.

11. If you have been sentenced to incarceration for a specified period of time, pray for those that must spend a lifetime in prison.

12. If you are about to lose everything you've ever owned, pray for those who have never owned anything.

14. If you are getting unbearably old, pray for those who will die unbelievably young.

15. You will perhaps someday go to heaven after all your suffering on earth, pray for those who suffer a lifetime on earth, then go on to an eternity in hell.

Lie #5: *"There's No Way Out!"*

Do you remember going through a house of mirrors at a carnival or state fair? If not, maybe you have seen one on television. Do you remember the excitement and fun of trying to find the way out, with people laughing and banging into mirrors in every direction? Laughing and enjoying the challenge of trying to get out of what seemed like an impossible maze was a fun part of the state fair.

Life is like that in many ways. When we are young, challenges and obstacles in our way hardly seem to bother us. It is generally as we grow older that we view the completion of a project or challenge as the only rewarding part. It is the "challenge" of getting out that seems to be such fun when we are young. The challenge of going through a house of mirrors can be fun. But if it took your entire lifetime to get out of one of those houses of mirrors, it would probably cease to be fun. Life is like that sometimes, too.

There is nothing fun about being in a situation where there seems to be an obstacle in every direction. Usually, it is not fun to see yourself in the mirror of life and to dislike what you see because you feel as if there is no way out. Satan is a master at building mazes and obstacles that can rob us of enjoyment and hope. If we choose to give up, Satan's illusions can even rob us of our will to live because it appears that we have no way out.

The "no way out" lie is probably not one we will hear from others as much as from inside our own minds and hearts.

In all honesty, there are times when there might not be an easy way out of a situation. There is a way out, however, perhaps even multiple ways out or through. More likely than not, difficult situations require difficult, yet possible, ways out. I remember an old pastor saying to the congregation, "There has never been a way in, that God didn't have a way out for His children." This was said three decades ago. These words speak truth to God's children. The way out is there for you. What matters is how you and I adjust ourselves to the situation.

Everything in our world is governed by laws of some kind. Physical things must act in ways that are governed by physical laws. It is the understanding of those laws that enables scientists to invent things once deemed "impossible" to build, make, or use.

Legal situations are governed by judicial laws. It is the understanding of judicial laws that enables legal experts to win "impossible" cases.

Medicine is governed by biological, chemical, and physical laws. It is the understanding of biological, chemical and physical laws that allows doctors and scientists to beat "impossible" odds and find cures for certain diseases.

Sinful humankind is also impacted by spiritual laws. By understanding and accepting spiritual laws in faith, humankind can repent, accept Jesus as Savior and Lord, and receive forgiveness.

Do you see a pattern developing here? The greatest path to the results you desire—your way out—is the understanding that comes from God through Jesus Christ.

Most of the time, however, understanding the way out of a situation will only come when we understand what has gotten us into the situation. Don't make a judgment about having "no way out" of your situation without knowing all of the facts. Just because you cannot see a way out of your situation doesn't mean there isn't a solution. Do you not know a way out? Don't give up without asking, researching, and learning. Leave no stone unturned!

Discreetly ask trusted Christians friends or church leaders if they have ever heard of a possible solution to your situation. Perhaps one of them knows about some organization(s) that can help people facing your situation. Seek Christian printed resources about a person or agency that can offer assistance with solutions to your problem.

Most of all, pray without ceasing for God to reveal a solution that is in His will! Ask God to grant you wisdom in seeking a way out or a way through. Study the Bible daily, searching for godly options to your situation. Pray day and night for a way out of the illusion of hopelessness that hovers over your circumstance. Without the illusion of hopelessness, the eventual, but often difficult, way out will, through God, become clear!

Bible Verses to Overcome Lie #5

- "Discretion shall preserve thee, understanding shall keep thee." Proverb 2:11 (KJV)

- "Thy word is a lamp unto my feet, and a light unto my path." Psalm 119:105 (KJV)

Related Scripture Passages

- Exodus 14
- Joshua 3, 4
- 1 Samuel 17
- Romans 8

Suggested Prayer Focus

1. Pray to God to give you inner peace and believe that there is an answer to your situation, even if you do not yet see or know the way out.

2. Ask God to help you make sound decisions in every aspect of your life. Pray that you will be equipped to arrive at a divinely inspired solution.

3. Pray for godly wisdom that will be a witness to others about the glory of God. Ask God to use you and your circumstances to inspire others.

4. Pray to recognize the thoughts, decisions, and actions that brought you to the point where you feel there is no way out.

5. Ask God to remove the hopelessness that is "blocking" your hope-laden vision.

6. Pray for divinely inspired judgment in all areas of your life.

7. Pray that Satan does not use fear and indecision to immobilize you so that you are rendered incapable of looking at available options.

8. Pray for open doors, open hearts, and windows of opportunity. Ask God to enhance your vision so that you can see the opportunities that come your way.

9. Pray for courage, strength, and stamina to survive the hard road you are travelling.

10. Ask God to lead you to the right friends and counselors for help.

11. Pray for your view of the challenges you face as being rewarding and constructive.

Steps to Take to Overcome Lie #5

1. Commit to spending your "free" time finding ways out of your situation.

2. Make an honest effort to determine the area of your spiritual life that you need to make the greatest change.

3. Identify the problem before you try to seek a solution.

4. Determine the actions that can begin or cease immediately that will bring you closer to finding a way out. Stop or start doing those things.

5. Research any facts and opportunities that will help you get out of this situation or overcome it. Be creative and don't let negative thinking stop you from exploring all options.

6. Realistically apply those facts to the resources you have available. (In other words, don't dream of attending a $50,000 therapy program in Switzerland when all you can afford is the $10 program at the YMCA. If this is true for you, take the $10 program and work hard, pray hard, train hard, and thank God for the program that has been made available to you.)

7. Establish daily, weekly, monthly, and yearly goals with the help of a "professional" in the area that you are having trouble. (For example, if you are having financial trouble, make a budget with advice from a financial counselor.)

8. Seek help that is affordable for you! Beware of scams and remember that just because something costs more, that doesn't mean it's better.

9. When you need to spend money in order to obtain help for your problem, find out what results are guaranteed before investing that

money. Make sure any "consultants," "counselors," and "advisors" are legitimate and that their practices, reputations and advice are aligned with Scripture. (No psychics, psychos, cons, or quacks!)

10. Seek trusted, qualified Christian counsel before signing a contract or making any long-term commitments or irreversible decisions.

Lie #6:
"Things Will Never Get Any Better!"

Can anything be further from the truth for a Christian? Things get better! If you have accepted Jesus Christ as Savior and Lord, someday things will be absolutely perfect!

Will that apply in this life on earth as it is now? No! And if someone has told you so, that, too, would be a hope-destroying lie because anytime you experienced trials and troubles you would lose all hope. Sound familiar?

So how does the promise of perfection in heaven affect you here on earth? In this way: the same God who created the heavens and earth; the same God who gave us life; the same God who gave His only Son to die for us; the same God who promised us the perfect heaven we so look forward to, promised us many other things that apply directly to life here on earth!

The Bible promises:

> Delight thyself also in the Lord, and he shall give thee the desires of thine heart. Commit thy way unto the Lord; trust also in him and he shall bring it to pass (Psalm 37:4-5).

Having the desires of your heart would mean things will get better, wouldn't it? But the first part of that promise comes before the second part. We must first delight ourselves in the Lord. We must first learn that true delight is in the Lord! When we do this, we are promised by God to have the desires of our heart! That would mean things will get better!

The Bible promises us:

When a man's ways please the Lord, he maketh even his enemies to be at peace with him" (Proverb 16:7).

Things would definitely get better if even your enemies were at peace with you! Please the Lord with your ways and rest assured because God will always honor His promises! Things will get better!

The Scriptures promise:

He that followeth after righteousness and mercy findeth life, righteousness, and honor"(Proverb 21:21).

Did you pay attention to the wonderful promise in the first part of that sentence? If you follow after righteousness, you will find it! When you find it, you will find life and honor! Would honor in your life make your life better and give you a feeling of hope?

Can wisdom help make things better in your life? Godly wisdom and grace can help you move beyond all of your past mistakes! Godly wisdom can help you make better decisions in the future. Making better decisions mean that things will get better in your life.

God's Word promises:

> "Happy is the man that findeth wisdom, and the man that getteth understanding" (Proverbs 4:13).

It's pretty obvious that if you were happy, things in your life would be better! Happy is good!

So how do you find wisdom? The answer, once again, can be found in God's Word:

> If any of you lack wisdom, let him ask of God, that giveth to all men liberally, and upbraideth not, and it shall be given him (James 1:5).

Ask for wisdom and God will give it to you!

Proverb 11:10 states:

> The fear of the LORD is the beginning of wisdom: a good understanding have all they that do his commandments.

When we pray and ask for wisdom, and when we read God's words and keep His promises, we are promised to find wisdom! Even our enemies will be at peace with us and we will gain happiness, and things will get better!

These are all promises from the same God—the one true God—who promises us the perfection of heaven! These are all promises for life on earth!

We will always have trials and troubles as long as we live; but if we have righteousness, life, honor, wisdom, happiness, and even peace with our enemies, things will get better! Read your Bible every day, pray without ceasing, and delight yourself in the Lord! The benefits will be great.

For those who truly serve Jesus with all of their lives, things will get better—not according to human interpretation, but according to what God knows is better! God promises!

Bible Verses to Overcome Lie #6

- "This I recall to my mind, therefore have I hope. It is of the Lord's mercies that we are not consumed, because his compassions fail not. They are new every morning: great is thy faithfulness." Lamentations 3:21-23 (KJV)

- "Surely goodness and mercy shall follow me all the days of my life: and I will dwell in the house of the Lord for ever." Psalm 23:6 (KJV)

Related Scripture Passages

- Luke 5:17-26
- Luke 21:1-38
- Revelation 21; 22:1-5
- Psalm 17

Suggested Prayer Focus

1. Ask God to reveal to you what it truly means to "delight thyself in the Lord," so that you may begin to do so.

2. Ask God to reveal to you what He desires from you as you commit yourself to Him fully.

3. In prayer, commit to God completely, even before you know exactly what God requires of you.

4. Pray for wisdom and understanding.

5. Pray that God will bestow upon you the faith that things will get better.

6. Ask God to help you recognize the difference between "pie in the sky" beliefs about a godly life here on earth and biblical promises of how things will get better.

7. Pray for patience to wait for things to get better as God works His divine will in your life.

8. Pray for peace, even while things are not better. God can grant you His peace which "passeth all understanding" (Philippians 4:7).

9. Pray for forgiveness if you have knowingly or unknowingly been selfish or spoiled about what God has or has not given to you.

Steps to Take to Overcome Lie #6

1. Write down a list of ways that your life could realistically change for the better within God's will. Keep in mind that God wants the best for you. The desires of your heart may be in keeping with His will for you.

2. Beside each point, identify those things that you believe God will expect you to take action on and do "your part" for making it better. Ask yourself if you have ignored you own responsibility to change your condition; or have you been waiting on God to do everything for you?

3. Identify the things that you recognize as being totally out of your control and solely in God's hands, requiring nothing but prayer from you. Commit to "staying out of God's way" and allow Him to work on those things that only He can change.

4. Commit to praying daily for everything on the list. Pray that God will give you trust and patience as He completes His work in you. Pray for courage and strength to take care of the things you need to do for yourself.

5. On the list of things that you can control, assign numbers to each one, prioritizing them according to most urgent changes needed.

6. From that prioritized list, make a "must do" work list for yourself.

7. If certain things must be accomplished by certain dates, mark those items with deadline dates. Set completion goal dates that are earlier than the actual deadline.

8. Place your list in an obvious place where you will see it every day.

9. Entertainment and recreation are important; however, recognize that there are times when we must change our priorities and sublimate our goals so that we can achieve what we desire. Commit to making whatever changes that are necessary for things to get better.

10. Start a "Journal of Changes" wherein you will keep track of all the steps you have taken toward making things better in your life.

11. In your journal, include every time you pray, every time you perform any work or action to make things better, every time you learn helpful information, and what that information is. Also include every time you recognize that God has changed something over which you had no control.

12. Thank and praise God daily for all changes.

13. Update your "must do" list daily.

14. Pray for guidance and help before you begin each new "must do" item on your list.

Lie #7:
"Good Christians Don't Have Problems!"

Is this the gospel according to fiction or according to Satan? Perhaps both. How can this be a lie? If it is a lie, how can this destroy your hope? It is a lie because it goes completely against what the Bible teaches. It can destroy hope because it gives millions of Christians false expectations, and ultimately a false sense of failure when those expectations aren't met.

If you have allowed this lie to get you down, you are not alone. Take heart, because you have not been tricked easily. It sounds so good and believable that many of us have been and continue to be affected by this lie!

Sometimes we know we have tried as hard as we can to serve the Lord and please Him. When we do, some of us may feel that nothing is supposed to go wrong during those times. As soon as things do go wrong, we feel like God didn't give us some reward He owed us, or we think, "What's the point of doing good or obeying God if things are still going to go wrong anyway?"

We immediately begin to lose hope, lose faith, and turn from the Bible and prayer, or even begin to question God. Why do we do that? We do it because we have fallen for a hope-destroying lie. The unique thing is that the belief that good Christians don't have problems may be one of the biggest lies that affects all believers. In fact, it is a lie that is probably never verbalized, although it is frequently, blatantly, and loudly implied.

Sometimes, through the innocent mishandling of Scripture, we are led to believe that good Christians never have trouble. On occasion, we are purposefully manipulated by "pie-in-the-sky" success messages that promise financial wealth, perfect health, and perfect human relationships for everyone.

We idolize the few wealthy and famous Christians of our time. We ask God, "Why not me?" But we never look at those worse off than us and ask God, "Why not me?"

How many times do we covet a steak dinner when there are those praying for a bowl of rice, or who are eating from garbage cans just to stay alive one more day?

We tend to pick out the verses of good fortune about those in Jesus' time and think, "Oh, how wonderful it would have been to walk with Jesus like the disciples did." But we never think, "Oh how wonderful it would have been to suffer for Christ's sake like many of the disciples did." We long to witness like John the Baptist, but we are not willing to eat bugs, live in the wilderness, and be decapitated because of such God-given witnessing power.

We dream only of the "wonderful" parts of modern-day testimonies and forget the nightmares that brought those testimonies about. Then we try to live up to our distorted view of what is supposed to happen when we attempt to live right.

Is being homeless a judgment of God claiming that He doesn't love you? Jesus said:

> The foxes have holes, and the birds of the air have nests; but the Son of man hath no where to lay his head (Matthew 8:20).

Does not owning a car mean you are not receiving God's blessings? Jesus never had the pleasure of riding in a car!

Is living with no air conditioning a disgrace or discomfort God has cursed you with? The Son of God never had one moment of air conditioning in His entire life on earth!

Is loneliness something you were promised that never happens to good Christians? What sin did Jesus commit for the loneliness He felt as He died on the cross?

If you are in a situation that is causing you great pain, dear precious servant of Jesus, those of us who have never walked a mile in your shoes cannot begin to imagine your pain. But Jesus Christ, the Holy Lamb, the King of Kings and Lord of Lords, feels your pain with you. He endured suffering for you. He sent the Holy Spirit to you.

When you earnestly dig into the Bible, you will find that much of what you considered to be a curse or punishment in spite of your efforts, in fact may be a heavenly measure of suffering that only true followers of Christ will suffer.

Perhaps because you are sharing the sufferings of Jesus for His sake, it would be appropriate for you to share His prayer to God:

> O my Father, if it be possible, let this cup pass from me: nevertheless not as I will, but as thou wilt (Matthew 26:39).

Bible Verses to Overcome Lie #7

- "Blessed are ye, when men shall revile you, and persecute you, and shall say all manner of evil against you falsely, for my sake. Rejoice, and be exceeding glad: for great is your reward in heaven: for so persecuted they the prophets which were before you." Matthew 5:11,12 (KJV)

Related Scripture Passages

- Acts 27—28
- Luke 22—24
- 2 Corinthians 11:22-33
- Matthew 14:1-12

Suggested Prayer Focus

1. Pray to see your time spent suffering on earth as just a tiny speck of time before the eternity you will spend in heaven.

2. Study to understand that the Bible does not teach "Good Christians will not have troubles."

3. Pray to realize that some troubles or events in life are just a part of life. They are not punishment, discipline, or chastisement from God. For example, aging, and its resulting effects, is not punishment. Work is not punishment. Accidents sometimes happen from carelessness or by no fault of your own, not as a judgment by God. Sickness and disease are the result of the Fall of Adam and Eve when they disobeyed God. Immorality was theirs, work was not on the agenda. Aging, bad health, and finally death came into the world because of what was done. Death is part of life and we must die before we can enter the kingdom of heaven.

4. Pray that God will remove any envy you might have toward those whom you believe "never" have anything bad happen to them.

5. Ask God to help you to realize there are no people who "never" have anything bad happen to them. Many times we don't know that people are experiencing difficulties because of their attitude toward their difficulties.

6. Pray to accept that righteousness is not always rewarded with earthly rewards, and earthly suffering is not always "deserved."

Steps to Take to Overcome Lie #7

1. Make a list of the names of all the Christians about whom you know personal information— but no more than ten persons. The names may include famous people whose personal testimony has been made public.

2. Beside each name, include one or more incidences of personal tragedy or hardship that each person had to endure. (This is not meant to be a listing of sins you believe they have committed. Rather, it is to be a list of problems, tragedies and dilemmas they have faced, regardless of whether the situation was the result of their own actions.

3. Think about the names of God's people in the Old Testament and the names of Christians in the New Testament and write them down on a sheet of paper. Beside each of those names or for some of them, write down all of the bad things that happened to them.

4. Watch the news every day for one week. Judging from the formula of one out of every two or three news stories, no matter how seemingly trivial or obviously tragic, we can deduce that Christians are not exempt from trials and tribulations.

5. Find out the capacity of every hospital in your area. Add the numbers together to determine

how many people in your area are likely to be in the hospital on any given day. Determine how many of them are likely to be Christians using the one-of-two or one-of-three method. Even if you assume that one-of-four patients are Christians, you still will find there are Christians with health problems. (Your answer will never equal zero!)

6. Talk to Christians who have endured through trials and tribulations. Ask them to share how they maintain strong faith in God during periods of trial and difficulty.

Lie #8:
"I'll Never Amount to Anything!"

This lie has probably been spoken out loud to people more than any of the other lies addressed in this book. The lies that destroy our self-esteem are lies we tell ourselves. This very hurtful lie is often told to us by others long before we begin to tell ourselves and believe in our own hearts, "I will never amount to anything."

Dear friend, because you have given your life to Jesus Christ, you are already somebody! You are privileged because you are a son or daughter of the God of the universe, our Heavenly Father!

You are a brother or sister and friend to the most precious Person who ever walked the face of the earth, Jesus, the Christ. You are the recipient of the greatest love in the universe. The Creator of the heavens and earth—King of all Kings, the One to whom all presidents, rich men and women, famous athletes, great warriors, and dignitaries will some-day bow down to—loves you just as you are right now, though He does not love your sin.

God is the Author and Finisher of all that you can become. God's will is the greatest and wisest of all! If you seek to do His will, God will help you try to accomplish it. After all, it is His will!

We know that because God is holy, perfect, just, loving, forgiving, and wise, and because He is Counselor, mighty, and omnipotent, God's plan is the best thing for your life! God does not make mis-takes. You are already something!

You are a wonderful part of a plan God developed long before the universe was formed. He sent His Son to die on the cross for you. He knew what you would be and can be, and what affect that could have on His will being accomplished on this earth. Your life has meaning and a purpose God will reveal to you!

If you will live your life for God, He will magnify His name through your life of submission to His will, the great perfect will for your life! In His will, you will be something wonderful!

God does not promise us that we will be rich; but if we are a wonderful part of His most perfect will, we can be many things.

You can be the faithful servant whose undying faith touches the heart of those who secretly watch your suffering. By your strength, they may be led to Jesus and His offer of eternal life in heaven!

You can be the survivor of such a horrific past that no one can imagine what you've overcome. You can be one whose life is a beacon of hope for many in the same situation!

You might be the prayer warrior who, on bended knee, causes the angels to sing great heavenly praises as they wonder in awe at your obedience to be faithful where you are!

Oh, my friend, how many hearts await you anxiously along the wonderful path God has for your life from this point forward—a path you have been on unknowingly all your life?

What does God have in store for you at this point in your life?

> And be not conformed to this world: but be ye transformed by the renewing of your mind, that ye may prove what is that good, and acceptable, and perfect, will of God (Romans 12:2).

If you do not conform to this world and let God renew your mind, you will demonstrate the good, acceptable, and perfect will of God for your life! Then you will not only know what good things God has already fashioned within you, you also will know the good things He wants you to be!

> And we know that all things work together for good to them that love God, to them who are called according to his purpose. For whom he did foreknow, he also did predestinate to be conformed to the image of his Son, that he might be the firstborn among many brethren. Moreover whom he did predestinate, them he also called: and whom he called, them he also justified: and whom he justified, them he also glorified. What shall we then say to these things? If God be for us, who can be against us? (Romans 8:28-31).

What will you be? If you walk with the Lord, you will be the one and only individual in the history of the world who can be the person God would have you be! Love God! Serve God! Live for God through Christ Jesus and be that person!

Bible Verses to Overcome Lie #8

- "Therefore if any man be in Christ, he is a new creature: old things are passed away; behold, all things are become new." 2 Corinthians 5:17 (KJV)

- "And Jesus said unto them, Come ye after me, and I will make you to become fishers of men." Mark 1:17 (KJV)

- "Commit thy works unto the LORD, and thy thoughts shall be established." Proverb 16:3 (KJV)

Related Scripture Passages

- Romans 6
- Luke 19:21-27
- Luke 22:24-27
- Philippians 4:4-23

Suggested Prayer Focus

1. Ask God to allow you to understand His love, beginning this very moment.

2. Pray to feel the presence of Jesus.

3. Ask God to remove from the forefront of your memory the voices of all those who told you hurtful things.

4. Pray to feel the Holy Spirit telling you the truth—that God loves you, that Jesus is hurting with you, and that God will give you His mercy and grace.

5. Pray to live like the new creature that you are in Christ.

6. Pray to witness the power of the victory promised to you in Christ.

7. Pray for the courage to forgive yourself for any sins for which you have already asked God's forgiveness.

8. Pray over any negative activity that is making you feel dirty, unworthy, unacceptable, or incapable to be removed.

9. Pray for the ability to forgive those who have caused you to feel like you are not an important person.

10. Pray to see yourself through God's love, just as He sees you.

Steps to Take to Overcome Lie #8

1. Make this an official, recognizable, memorable, documented, life-changing moment in your life, wherein you agree with God that you will, through Jesus, daily Bible reading, and prayer discover and believe that, "I will be something."

2. Do that through prayer right now where you are, or at a place that will be special and memorable to you. (Don't let Satan distract you, though, by spending so much time finding "just the right place" that you never do it.) It's the commitment in your heart, not the place that matters most.

3. Record that moment in your Bible. Write down the date, time, and place that moment occurred. Record enough information so that you will never forget it, but omit any private thoughts that might embarrass you if read by others.

4. Begin to evaluate the friendships, family relations, acquaintances, work relationships and situations, etc., that make you feel like you will never become a person of self-worth.

5. When possible and within God's will, remove yourself from those situations. Pray for those people in Christian love.

6. Seek friendships and relationships that support and encourage you and help you understand that you are somebody. Seek God's strength to help you accept and believe their positive statements about yourself.

7. Do not expose yourself to movies, television, radio programs, music, reading materials, environments, or activities that cause you to believe you are guilty, incapable, or inadequate.

8. Find and participate in as many positive Christian programs for self-improvement, self-empowerment, or community service projects as you can. Through helping others you can give yourself a greater sense of accomplishment.

9. Constantly study, learn and receive any education, training or work experience, within God's will, that will help you advance in some area of your life. Work for improvement not recognition.

10. Put all of your heart and soul into serving God. Trust Him to make you the person He wants you to be.

11. Study, work hard and train hard for the task you believe God would have you to accomplish. Avoid striving for accomplishment simply to impress others.

Lie #9:
"God Has Turned His Back on Me!"

Do you feel as though God has turned His back on you? Then who do you suppose arranged for you to get this message? Does Satan call people to listen for the still small voice of God, inviting them to forgiveness? You are being called to listen for that voice.

Do Satan's demons call Christians to walk as Jesus taught and enjoy the awesome wonder of life with God? Of course not! You are being called to walk as Jesus taught and enjoy the awesome wonder of life with God.

Who reached out to humanity by sending His only Son to die for them, by saving them, and welcoming them home with undying love when they have given up on Him? Only God can do that—through Jesus, through the Holy Spirit—served by someone and some circumstances that allowed you to find this message of hope through Jesus Christ!

Satan does not stand against Satan to defeat Satan. You are reading this now because God has not given up on you! Satan wants you to believe that God has turned His back on you when, in fact, you are turning your back on God. How can that be known, when your situation is not known?

No matter what your current situation, if you are Christian, you would not be hearing the voice of Satan over the voice of God. If you believe in Him, you will hear His voice only, unless you have taken your eyes off Jesus and turned your back on God. Who has spoken to you in the loudest voice lately?

God is calling you this very moment to remember the faith you placed in Him at the moment of your conversion! God is calling you to remember the saving grace He lovingly gave to you when you didn't deserve it.

God is calling you to remember the precious blood of His Son, Jesus, when He died on the cross. God is calling you to remember the victory that Jesus had over Satan, sin, and death when He gloriously arose from the grave!

God is calling you to remember all of the wonderful promises of the Bible—the hope of glory in heaven, the golden streets, and the promise of eternity in heaven, the promises of guidance, strength, sufficient grace, and hope right here on earth!

Is it possible to know all of those things and dare to look to the God of the universe and say He has turned His back on you? Are you angry with God? Dear friend, you should fall to your knees this very moment and beg God for forgiveness. But, as mighty and powerful as God is, even as King of the Universe, He doesn't require you to kneel right now. You can stand right where you are. He will hear you and He will forgive you.

God longs to have a relationship with you. He longs to feel your love for Him. But, more importantly, He longs for you to feel His love again.

God has sustained you, no matter how terrible your circumstances seem, to enjoy the fellowship of God and His love. God longs to comfort you.

His heart yearns for you to walk with Jesus as you did on the day you gave your life to Him.

If by chance you are reading this message and you have never given your life to Jesus Christ and asked Him to be your Savior and Lord, it is God's will that you do so now. The Bible says it is not God's will that anyone should perish (2 Peter 3:9). It also says no man cometh unto the Father but by the Son (John 14:6). Have you done that?

As you consider your relationship with God, remember the Bible says in 1 John 1:9,10:

> If we confess our sins, he is faithful and just to forgive us our sins, and to cleanse us from all unrighteousness. If we say that we have not sinned, we make him a liar, and his word is not in us.

God's Word also promises in 2 Chronicles 7:14:

> If my people, which are called by my name, shall humble themselves, and pray, and seek my face, and turn from their wicked ways; then will I hear from heaven, and will forgive their sin, and will heal their land. (KJV)

God does not turn His back on you. He gave the world His Son, Jesus, to prove everything! If you turn your face to God now, you will not see His back. You will see His open arms!

Bible Verses to Overcome Lie #9

- And David said to Solomon his son, Be strong and of good courage, and do it: fear not, nor be dismayed: for the LORD God, even my God, will be with thee; he will not fail thee, nor forsake thee, until thou hast finished all the work for the service of the house of the LORD. 1 Chronicles 28:20 (KJV)

- Be strong and of a good courage, fear not, nor be afraid of them: for the LORD thy God, he it is that doth go with thee; he will not fail thee, nor forsake thee. Deuteronomy 31:6 (KJV)

Related Scripture Passages

- Daniel 3
- Luke 4:16-30
- Psalm 23
- John 15

Suggested Prayer Focus

1. Pray for the wall of sin, doubt, or faithlessness in your life to be removed from you so that you can understand that God has not turned His back on you.

2. Humble yourself in prayer as God has directed in Scripture.

3. Seek His face with your heart in prayer.

4. Confess your sins and repent. Ask God to forgive your sins.

5. Ask God to reveal sins you are not aware of and heal your life.

6. Ask God to remove all other negative or unholy thoughts from your mind and heart.

7. Ask God to relentlessly pursue you and mold you until you will never turn from Him.

8. Ask God to bring you to spiritual maturity that recognizes His presence in all situations, regardless of appearances.

Steps to Take to Overcome Lie #9

1. Read one new Psalm each morning, noon, and night until you have completed reading the entire Book of Psalms.

2. If you still believe God has turned His back on you, read them all again. Repeat the process for as long as you have doubt.

3. Obtain a copy of the New National Baptist Hymnal with permission, and sing your favorite hymns to yourself.

4. Go to the sanctuary of your church at a time when you can be there alone. Sit alone and listen with your heart for God to speak to you.

5. Go to the altar and leave your concerns there with God, even if you are not sure what is bothering you.

6. Commit to watching and/or listening only to Christian programs and reading only Christian material that is in keeping with God's Word.

7. Study your Bible for verses you have high-lighted, marked, or in any way found significant at some other point in life.

8. Call or visit friends whom you know are very close to the Lord at this point in their lives. Share your concerns with them.

9. Seek counsel from your pastor or a qualified Christian counselor.

10. Make a list of all the tragedies that could have happened to you but didn't; thank and praise God for the freedom from them.

11. Have daily prayer sessions in which you pray for the needs of others—anyone's and every-one's but your own.

12. Sit in an emergency waiting room for several hours when you are not there for yourself. Pray for those who are there for health emergencies.

13. If you are a patient in the hospital, spend all of your time praying for the needs and salvation of other patients and staff.

14. Write a letter to Jesus and tell Him about all of the things His Father has done for you in your life. Mail it to yourself and, when you get it, read it and imagine how Jesus would feel reading those words. Pray to God just to talk with Him and listen to Him.

15. Attend church every time there is a worship service, even when you do not feel like it.

Lie #10: *"Suicide Is the Only Way Out!"*

Suicide is the irreversible, wrong solution to life's problems and Satan's most malignant lie of all! No matter how terrible your conditions are right now, your situation does not compare to the conditions that await those who will burn in hell forever.

Did you know if you die right now and have not given your life to Jesus Christ, these conditions and worse are waiting for you?

The Bible says in Revelation 20:15:

> And whosoever was not found written in the book of life was cast into the lake of fire. (KJV)

If you have never given your life to Jesus Christ, repented of your sin, and accepted Him as Lord, you can know beyond a shadow of a doubt that this is what awaits you after you draw your last breath here on earth.

The Bible also says of hell in Mark 9:48:

> Where their worm dieth not, and the fire is not quenched.

If you went to hell right now, you would spend eternity burning in darkness, separated from God with no chance of repentance, with worms that would forever eat his or her flesh and never die. Are you on fire right now as you are reading this? Is your body right now literally engulfed in flames that won't stop? Are worms eating your flesh right this moment—not just ordinary worms but worms that never die? Are they eating your flesh right this moment as you scream into a darkness darker than you've ever known? Probably not! Surely nothing that you are facing currently is as what you would face in hell. Whatever your conditions are now, Satan wants to trick you into believing suicide is the answer.

The Bible says of heaven in Revelation 21:27:

And there shall in no wise enter into it any thing that defileth, neither whatsoever wor-keth abomination, or maketh a lie: but they which are written in the Lamb's book of life.

God's Word clearly teaches that eternal sepa-ration from God, and eternity in hell, await those who are not in Christ. If you have even the slightest doubt about your salvation, suicide would be an irreversible mistake with horrible eternal consequences!

If you are unsaved and feeling suicidal, you need to pray and ask God to give you the courage to stay alive so that you can find out how to truly give your life to Jesus so you can spend eternity in heaven with God, instead of eternally separated from Him! Then you need to go about living for Jesus!

If you are sure about your salvation, you need to begin to pray without ceasing, because suicidal thoughts do not come from heaven! God gives great hope to anyone who accepts Jesus as Lord and then asks for hope!

Jesus died and paid for all sins you have committed! His death, burial, and resurrection guarantee hope to all believers, even in the most terrible conditions, and even in your situation! If you're not saved, Satan wants you to die thinking that you are. Jesus does not advocate suicide! Hear Him!

Jesus loves you so much! He is calling you right now to live your life for Him! He wants to give you such glorious hope and love that it is beyond human comprehension. He knows what is in your future and He longs to show you what that wonderful future holds in store for you!

Jesus loves you and He wants you to live an abundant life on this earth. He has a purpose for you that will put everyone in awe of the changes He has for your life!

Pray to Jesus right this second to save your life! Pray for help. Ask Him save you from your suicidal thoughts. Pray for hope. You are only one prayer away from taking the first steps to changing your entire life forever.

Pray immediately for a hedge of protection around your life! Pray for God to remove Satan"s demonic activity from around you! Pray that He will cleanse your thoughts. Ask Jesus to forgive you of all your sins and give Him control of your life.

The hope that you have prayerfully pleaded for is waiting for you to accept as a free gift now! Pray for that hope and receive it! Pray that you can look beyond your presence circumstances to see hope for your future.

Jesus loves you! Pray and ask Him to help you feel His overflowing love for you. Jesus loves you! Pray to have the assurance of His love. Jesus loves you! Pray to know the hope that His love brings to you. Jesus loves you! Thank Him for His unending love. Jesus loves you! Praise Him for His sacrifices and suffering for your sake. Jesus loves you! Open you heart to feel the joy that comes from His love. Jesus loves you! You have much to live for!

Bible Verses to Overcome Lie #10

- "For God so loved the world, that he gave his only begotten Son, that whosoever believeth in him should not perish, but have everlasting life." John 3:16 (KJV)

- "For God sent not his Son into the world to condemn the world; but that the world through him might be saved." John 3:17 (KJV)

Related Scripture Verses

- John 3
- Revelation 20:12-15
- Matthew 12:28-30
- Ephesians 6:10-20

Suggested Prayer Focus

1. If you or someone you know are having suicidal thoughts, immediately call a suicide hotline, a prayer line, or a qualified counselor while you pray to God in your heart for an immediate and absolute hedge of protection. Pray about all of the following items:

2. Pray and ask God to immediately remove Satan, his evil messages, and all demonic activity from you or the person contemplating suicide.

3. Pray to feel Jesus' presence with you that it may give you peace.

4. Pray for God's angels to surround you (or your friend) and stay away from anything that can harm the body or the spirit.

5. Pray for a sound mind and calm spirit.

6. Pray for God to send someone to help you immediately and to counsel you (or your friend).

7. Tell God that you (or your friend) accept Jesus' forgiveness. Belief in His forgiveness yields hope.

8. Resist Satan in Jesus' name. Stay away from anything that is ungodly. The Bible says to resist the devil and he will flee (James 4:7).

9. Praise God for being there to save you. (The Bible says God inhabits the praise of His people Ephesians 2:22).

Steps to Take to Overcome Lie #10

1. Immediately pray for God's help while you pick up a telephone and call a suicide hotline, a qualified counselor, or even 911.

2. Do everything they tell you to do when they tell you to do it. Don't allow arrogance or embarrassment to keep you from getting help.

3. Stay on the phone with the counselor until help arrives, unless you are instructed otherwise by the counselor.

4. Continue to pray to God in your heart as you do what the counselor advises.

5. Do not take medication in any manner other than prescribed for you by a physician, or as the non-prescription label indicates.

6. Do not pick up or go near any item which can harm you.

7. Do not go near any area where you can harm yourself.

8. Ignore any voices (or tell your friend to ignore them) that tell you to kill yourself. Those voices are not from God, Jesus, the Holy Spirit, angels, or anything godly. A message to take your own life comes directly from Satan.

9. When you (or your friend) survive an episode of suicidal thoughts, seek professional Christian

counseling immediately. Praise and thank God for deliverance in that very moment.

10. If you are afraid or embarrassed to seek professional counseling to the point you will not do it, contact your pastor or anyone you know who will immediately help you arrange for professional counseling. Remember that you are not alone. Many people have been besieged by suicidal thoughts. Every person is worthy of help and every life is worth saving. There are committed, trained professionals who want to help you.

11. Follow all advice from your professional counselor. Stay in counseling until you have worked through the issue(s) that caused you to feel the need to take your own life.

Lie #11:
"I'm Powerless to Do Anything About It!"

When you think of this lie, think of a great big human-sized jelly-fish. That's what Satan would have us think about our roles in life—that we all just float through the ocean of life like a bunch of spineless, spiritual jelly-fish!

This kind of thinking can be built on ideas that fit into one of two major categories. The first one suggests that everything is based on luck, "karma," good vs. bad energy, voodoo, astrology, evolution, or any number of secular (worldly) ideas. Most of these ideas generate from people who have no understanding or saving knowledge of God and Jesus Christ.

The second category of the "jelly-fish" concept of life comes from people who know God and believe, "If God is in charge of everything, then there's nothing I can do to affect the outcome of my life. God already knew when the universe was spoken into existence what I was going to do and be, and there's nothing I can do about it."

That version sounds more believable because it mentions God and recognizes His omniscience (He knows all things), and His omnipotence (He is all powerful).

The problem with all of the "jelly-fish" concepts that say, "Everything is out of our control," is that they are absolute lies! They do not line up with what the Bible teaches!

The secular approaches to humanity's role in life do not even acknowledge God as God. They suggest that luck determines our way, and that no one has control over luck, not even God! They suggest that "karma," energy, the stars, or "mother earth" are in control of our lives. The secular approach never considers the question: "Who created the earth, the moon, the stars, and everything in the universe and Adam and Eve?"

Sometimes these concepts of our place in life are obviously wrong to Christians because they do not mention God. At times, even well-meaning Christians fall prey to these lies.

More likely than that, though, Christians fall prey to the "jelly-fish" concepts that at least mention God. But what does the Bible really teach about us having some control over our own lives?

From the very first book of the Bible, Genesis, to the very last book, Revelation, we see that humankind has much control over our fate in every part of life. Not control over everything that happens, but control over how to react to it.

In Genesis, we see that when God made Adam and Eve in the garden of Eden, God did not make brainless, mindless puppets on strings. He gave them both a soul, and a brain, and permission to make decisions, right or wrong, that each man and woman can use to react to physical and spiritual laws here on earth.

God has given all individuals who ever have or ever will walk the earth control over whether they would choose right or wrong, good or evil, life or death!

In Revelation, we see how each person's control over accepting or rejecting Jesus Christ and the teachings of God in the Bible affect that individual's eternal destination.

God is in control of the universe, and ultimately everything in it. In His infinite wisdom, however, He saw fit to give us control over many things in our lives. He controls the universe and all its spiritual and physical laws, but we are allowed to be in total control of how we react to it.

Satan wants us to believe that our reactions to our circumstances are all out of our control so that we will float through life like spineless jelly-fish.

Scripture proves that we have much control over our fate when it says:

> That we henceforth be no more children, tossed to and fro, and carried about with every wind of doctrine, by the sleight of men, and cunning craftiness, whereby they lie in wait to deceive" (Ephesians 4:14).

We can, through the power of Jesus Christ, control whether or not we are tossed about! As a matter of fact, the Bible teaches that we are accountable for the control we have exercised over gifts, talents, and opportunities that the Holy Spirit gives to us through belief in Christ!

God wants us to recognize that we are not in control of many things; however, we are in control of how we react to anything and everything that happens in this world! Praise God and His Son, Jesus... it's not all out of their control!

Bible Verses to Overcome Lie #11

- "And he called him, and said unto him, How is it that I hear this of thee? give an account of thy stewardship; for thou mayest be no longer steward." Luke 16:2 (KJV)

- "The ants are people not strong, yet they prepare their meat in the summer." Proverb 30:25 (KJV)

- God is my strength and power: and he maketh my way perfect. He maketh my feet like hinds' feet: and setteth me upon my high places. 2 Samuel 22:33-34 (KJV)

Related Scripture Passages

- Proverbs 10
- Proverbs 11
- Proverbs 12
- Proverbs 13

Suggested Prayer Focus

1. Admit to God in prayer that you recognize God-given control over many areas in your life.

2. Ask for forgiveness for blaming God for things over which He has given you control.

3. Pray for forgiveness from self-pity and ask God to remove it.

4. Pray for the removal of "jelly-fish'" type beliefs that make us believe that circumstances are all out of our control.

5. Ask God to reveal to you that He is ultimately in control of everything in the universe, while at the same time, giving us much control over decisions, choices, and reactions in life.

6. Ask God to help you understand the things you are in control of and things over which you have no control.

7. Pray for God to strengthen your faith and trust in Him for things over which He does not allow you any control.

8. Pray to recognize when you are "wrestling" with God for control over something He does not want you to control.

9. Ask God each morning for guidance in the areas over which He has given you control.

Steps to Take to Overcome Lie #11

1. Begin carrying a small notebook or note pad everywhere you go. Use it to make a journal of every decision you make, no matter how small

or large. Every time you get to make a choice, log that opportunity to exercise some control and what your choice was.

2. Make entries also for every significant reaction you have to events that were not in your control. For example, when things go badly or differently than you expect or hope, do you react calmly, coolly, wisely, and maturely Christian? Or do you get angry, pout and whine, or give up?

3. Every evening, just before you go to bed, review the choices you made that day, and the reactions you had to the events. Beside each of those choices, make a note of any bad results that could have happened or did happen because of the control you exercised in the situation.

4. Write the words: "I had some control over this situation," beside that entry.

5. Continue this process for one month. Doing so for one month allows for a wide variety of situations over which you have some control, from hourly to daily, weekly to monthly and even some things over which you have control that will affect your life for years.

6. Each night, after you review your journal entries, thank God for the control He has given you. Ask for forgiveness for the control you have abused. Praise Him for His power and His

willingness to help you recover from situations in which you were irresponsible.

7. Every time you catch yourself asking God, "Why did you let this happen to me?" stop that thought immediately, and surrender it to God. Replace that thought with, "God, please reveal to me anything I did or did not do that could have prevented this."

8. When you are struggling with control, repeat the Serenity Prayer, as written by Reinhold Niebuhr (1951):

> God, grant me the serenity
> to accept the things
> I cannot change;
>
> Courage to change
> the things I can; and the
> wisdom to know the difference.

Lie #12:
"I've Got It All Under Control!"

Can thinking, "I've got it all under control," really destroy your hope? What negative thing could possibly happen because you believe that you are in control of every aspect of your life?

Major negative things could happen at two opposite extremes of your life if you believe the lie that you are in control of everything.

If you are currently experiencing trouble in your life, the first thing to remember is that this is a low point in your life. If circumstances are such that you believe everything has gone wrong in your life, and you believe you once were in control of every single aspect of your life, you may put undue, unbearable pressure on yourself for events over which you actually had no control in the first place!

If you start to feel overwhelmed by circumstances you cannot control, it will be hard for you to see hope for change to occur in your life. As you think about facing, and attempting to overcome those same circumstances, accept that there is no room for hope in the areas you personally cannot change. In life, you will find that there are such areas.

God has given human beings control over many of the aspects and areas of our lives, but there are areas that we absolutely cannot control and never will! There are areas that God recognizes will help us more if He allows us to make mistakes and learn from them. In those areas, God gives us control, no matter how right or wrong our choices may be!

At the same time, God in His infinite wisdom recognizes there are areas of our lives—individually and collectively as part of the human race—that are better left in His complete control! Those are the things we cannot control.

We begin to lose all hope when we get the two areas mixed up! For example, let's say you are in a situation that you caused. If you caused the situation by a certain action that was within your control, you could accept responsibility for your actions and prepare for different choices, actions, and results in the future.

You can maintain hope for the future with the understanding that you will try not to make the same mistake. By recognizing what God allows you to control, you will not "blame" God, ruin your relationship with Him, and lose your hope.

Likewise, if you are involved in a situation for which you are not responsible, you should not consider that you have failed, blame yourself, and get depressed, wondering why you allowed yourself to fail. If you did all you could (within God's will) to avoid the circumstance, and it still happened, God does not hold you accountable or guilty! You can know not to get down on yourself.

In that bad situation (wherein you know God was in complete control and you had no control), you can know that there is only one place to turn for consolation, understanding, strength, help, and hope—turn to God through Jesus Christ. If you give your life to Him, even in the worst situation you will have hope by knowing what you can control, and what things over which God has not given you control.

The second set of extremes that can cause a negative thing to happen from believing "I've got it all under control," are the extremely good times of your life. If you believe life is great just because you have total control over what happens to you, you are setting yourself up for a great fall!

God deserves all the glory, praise, and credit for the good things in our lives, even when He has required us to put forth effort to see that good thing come about! When we fail to recognize God's handiwork in our lives, we lose the close relationship with God that we need to truly enjoy life.

If we turn our backs on God, we will begin to feel a great void that only He can fill. We lose the close walk and wisdom that we enjoyed to the point of success, then we began to live foolishly. We then fail, falling flat on our faces and setting in motion the cycle of loss of hope, self-blame, and confusion!

God, in His loving kindness, will prevent that cycle when we use daily Bible reading, fervent prayer and a close walk with Jesus Christ to point out the things we so obviously can control, and things God has graced us not to worry about!

Bible Verses to Overcome Lie #12

- "I am the vine, ye are the branches: He that abideth in me, and I in him, the same bringeth forth much fruit: for without me ye can do nothing" John 15:5 (KJV).

- "The Lord maketh poor, and maketh rich: he bringeth low, and lifteth up" 1 Samuel 2:7 (KJV).

Related Scripture Passages

- Luke 12:16-21
- Psalm 18
- Psalm 25
- Psalm 37

Suggested Prayer Focus

(If you are at a "low point" in life and feeling that you are without hope.)

1. Pray for God to grant you peace about things you did not cause but might feel guilty about.

2. Pray for Jesus to carry your burdens. Lay them down at the throne of grace and leave them there. He will pick them up for you. Pray for rest.

3. Pray for peace about unchangeable events or conditions in your life, country, and world

4. Pray for God to address the areas of life that you cannot.

(If you are at a "high point" but are still feeling that you are without hope.)

1. Thank and praise God for all of the good things in your life and give all glory and credit to Jesus and to the Father.

2. Pray for humility before the Lord and for a humble spirit before others.

3. Ask for wisdom, guidance, prudence, and continued faith.

4. Pray that you will be accepting of the turns of events in God's will.

Steps to Take to Overcome Lie #12

Like the person who believes, "It is all out of my control," you will need to keep a journal that helps you to distinguish between the things that are in your control and the things that are not.

Whether you are at a low point and believing it is all in your control and "all my fault," or at a high point and believing, "I did this all myself," your steps to see the truth are very easy.

(If you are at a low point in life, yet "working your hardest.")

1. Carry a notebook or journal to make entries of every situation or event you encounter that is out of your control.

2. Make an entry for all weather conditions that hinder you.

3. Make an entry for every single decision made by someone else that affects you negatively but you could not avoid.

4. Write down every law or rule you must follow that hinders an honest means of succeeding.

5. Make a list of every mechanical failure you couldn't avoid.

6. Make one for every bad event or thing you did your best to avoid, but it happened anyway.

7. Each night before you go to bed, praise God entry by entry for using those people, conditions, and events for strengthening you for the future. Pray for all those people.

8. Thank and praise God for not holding you responsible for those things. Pray for strength to overcome. Pray for faith.

(*If you are at a high point in life, because you "did it all."*)

1. Make an entry for the weather when you benefit from it.

2. Make an entry for every time you travel in your car and another motorist doesn't swerve to hit you head on.

3. Make one for every meal you eat that was provided by someone else's farming ability.

4. Make an entry for every day that you do not suffer tragedy.

5. Make one for every choice made by someone else that profits you—a choice you had nothing to do with.

6. Make an entry for every day that you are not victimized by someone with evil intentions.

7. Make an entry for every day that your heart continues to beat and your body functions, allowing you to do the things you need to do.

8. Praise God for every entry. Ask for forgiveness for human pride and arrogance.

Lie #13:
"I Am a Failure!"

You are not a failure! People are not failures; people have failures! Everybody has them! The word "failure" just means "failing to perform an expected action!" It is a measurement of an expected action, not a measurement intended for people. The word failure, according to Webster's Dictionary, didn't even appear in the English language until about 400 years after the word fail!

That means for at least 400 years, people were able to recognize that fact—we could acknowledge when some action or event failed to happen, without viewing anyone as being a failure.

So if failing supposedly makes someone a failure, and everyone fails sometimes, then that would mean that everyone is a failure! Do you believe that? You shouldn't! It's not true! And it is also not true that you personally are a failure.

Maybe you're thinking, "Yeah, everybody may have one or two failures in their whole life, but I'm a failure because I've had more blunders than anyone I know!"

Do you know who Thomas Edison is? He is considered one of the most successful inventors and scientists of all time, but he failed in his first 10,000 attempts to invent a working light bulb! That figure is not an exaggeration. He actually tried 10,000 times before he had a working bulb. But Edison is by no means considered a failure! Have you literally failed 10,000 times at any one thing? No? Then you are not a failure!

Do you believe that you "strike out" at everything you try to accomplish? Babe Ruth struck out more than any baseball player in his time, and he was never considered a failure. He just kept swinging until he had more home-runs than anyone up to and including his lifetime!

What about scriptural examples of people who failed in really big ways, but who to this day are not considered failures? Are there biblical examples of God using people who failed? Of course, there are! Was God able to do wonderful things through their lives and actions? Of course, He was!

Moses, chosen by God to lead His people, failed God in a great way by murdering a man in anger. God was still able to do many, many great things in Moses' life. Moses personally failed God on several other important occasions as well. Yet no one who believes in God's Word would ever call Moses a failure.

Peter literally denied Jesus three times during the most trying time of Jesus' life. God did not consider Peter a failure whom God could not restore. Peter failed Jesus that day and failed to continue Jesus' work for a while after Jesus' crucifixion and resurrection. God still did not treat Peter as a failure. Instead, He used Peter to do even more things for the kingdom.

The prodigal son in Matthew 15 failed so utterly and completely that he ended up dining with pigs. Jesus used that story as an example of how eager God is to welcome us back from failure and sin and to restore us to a right relationship with Him.

Remember these five very important truths about failure:

1. Failure means "not performing an expected action." It is not a measure of a person's worth. The Bible says all human beings fall short (fail).

2. You cannot judge yourself as a failure without calling God a failure as well. God is not through with you yet, and God absolutely cannot fail!

3. God has worked many great things through people with tragic failures in their lives!

4. God can overcome all of your failures, if you allow Him to, and empower you to serve Him for His honor and glory.

5. People are not failures. Only their actions can be counted as failures.

Before you look too hard at any failure you have experienced, ask yourself whose expectations you were trying to live up to—yours or God's? Ask if those expectations were realistic, considering all the ways the Bible teaches us to prepare for challenges?

Did you try to succeed on your own, or did you prepare in accordance with Scripture?

Are you prayed up, studied up, seeking God's will, and walking with Jesus? When you are in this mode, you will be victorious—even in failure—by living in God's will through Jesus Christ!

Bible Verses to Overcome Lie #13

- "I can do all things through Christ which strengtheneth me." Philippians 4:13 (KJV)

- "Nay, in all these things we are more than conquerors through him that loved us." Romans 8:37 (KJV)

Related Scripture Passages

- Luke 15
- 2 Samuel 11—12
- Matthew 26
- Exodus 2

Suggested Prayer Focus

1. Ask for forgiveness of your sin in those times when your failure was a sin.

2. Claim the right God gave you to come boldly before the throne of grace, asking for help in Jesus' name to recover from failure.

3. Pray to recognize that Jesus is your Advocate when failure challenges you.

4. Praise God that He does not consider you to be a failure and ask Him to let that truth sink into your heart and mind.

5. Praise God for making human beings with free will and that it is possible for us to fail and make mistakes as a result of His perfect wisdom, understanding, design, and will.

6. Praise God for choosing men and women in the Bible to serve Him greatly and mightily after they had previously failed Him.

7. Praise God for sharing the truth of their failure with us in the Bible. Ask God to call to your mind their failures as lessons for you.

8. Ask God to block from your mind thoughts that cause you to consider yourself a failure.

9. Praise God that He already recognizes that you will fail again, just like everyone else, and that He still loves you and longs to use you to serve Him through the power and might of Jesus Christ.

Steps to Take to Overcome Lie #13

1. Write a list of all your favorite men and women from the Bible.

2. Study the Scriptures to find all of the stories in the Bible about those people.

3. For each name, make a list of all the things you would consider as failure in that person's life.

4. Commit to memory all of those failures and remember that these persons are still your favorite people from the Bible.

5. Write a list of all the ways God used each of these persons after their failures.

6. Go to your church library, local library, or Christian bookstore, and find books and other materials that will help you learn the life stories of all your modern-day Christian heroes and heroines.

7. Make a list of every failure those persons recognize or claim as failure.

8. Make a list of everything they did that you would consider to be failure, if it had happened to you.

9. Listen to testimonies at your church, or on radio or television, about people who have failed, but whom God has chosen to use after their failures.

10. Think of the person you love more than anyone else in the whole world and would not want anyone to call that person a failure.

11. Make a list (even if only in your mind) of the setbacks and defeats that you know the person you love has experienced in his or her life.

Think about why you still love that person in spite of his or her failure.

12. Every time you believe you are a failure, tell yourself the same things you believe Jesus would tell your best friend or loved one if they failed in the same way or ways you have.

13. Make a list of every success and accomplishment you have made in your life. Do not look down on the failures you made when you were younger. They were, more than likely, age-appropriate mistakes. Keep the list and add to it every time you think of a new failure. Reread the definition of failure.

14. Ask God to call to your memory all of the successes you have had. Write them down on a sheet of paper. Remember even the smallest victories in your life. Praise God for each victory in your life.

15. Compare your lists to determine whether your successes outnumber your failures. If they do not, be sure that you are not indulging in negative thinking and blocking yourself from acknowledging successes in your life.

Lie #14:
"My Finances Are Hopeless!"

Saying that "There is not enough money," is not the same as saying, "There is no hope." Satan would have us think that the two statements are related. According to the Bible, however, your true hope is not dependent upon having enough money to do all of the things that you want or need to do.

There are plenty of biblical laws and instructions that will help us avoid situations where there are more bills than money to pay them. But where do we find our hope when we find ourselves on the bad side of debt?

Does hope come only when we know that eventually our bills will be paid? Does hope come only when we find a "miracle cure" or "sure-fire guarantee" program for our financial ailments? That's what Satan would have us to believe.

But in whom or in what are you placing your hope when the only hope and peace you can see lies in paying off your debts? At that point, is your hope placed in Jesus Christ or in the money or plan that guarantees the payment of the debt?

If you can only find hope in the fact that God will show you how to pay your debts, you are placing your hope in the wrong thing. Your hope needs to be absolutely in God through Jesus Christ, not in the comfort that God will guarantee your debts will eventually be paid.

What if you had just survived a medical catastrophe with bills in the hundreds of thousands, or even millions of dollars? What if you were left in a physical condition that makes it almost impossible for you to earn that amount of money?

If that were true, and you had placed all of your hope in paying those debts off "somehow, some day," your hope would still not really in be in Jesus Christ. Satan can quickly and effortlessly rob that kind of hope with just one look at your latest hospital bill.

If you want true hope that is unaffected by your financial situation, your hope must be in Jesus Himself, not in any guaranteed pay-off plan you believe He will provide! Does that mean God won't provide wisdom and instruction on how to approach your debts? No! God has already provided volumes of instruction and wisdom that will help you to face your financial obligations in the best possible way on earth. Much can be learned from reading the Bible, but much of it will come through prayer, Bible study, personal commitment to follow biblical instruction on debt, and biblical instruction for daily living!

That instruction is a "secondary," extra benefit to living right with Jesus. Your hope and peace will come from Jesus Himself. Your hope will come in knowing that Jesus loves you, and He promises to see you through any situation you will ever be faced with on earth, including great debts!

Does that mean that God will enable you to pay the debt? It might; but it might not. God desires for you to do the best you can with what you have been given.

If you truly trust Jesus with all your heart, you will have peace and hope, no matter what. That means of your hope will be independent of the results, and that Satan cannot rob you of your hope in that way.

If you are faithful to follow the instruction God has provided in the Bible for handling debt, the instruction for how to approach work, the instruction for facing the unavoidable, the instruction for living victoriously in adversity, and the instruction on how to seek and find wisdom, you will find God-given hope through Jesus Christ. Then, and only then, will you be able to find true peace and hope against all odds! Then, and only then, will you see the hope God has already put in place and in motion for you to survive any crushing debt you might be facing!

Will God provide any help with your debt? Of course, but it doesn't mean He's going to drop miracle money out of the sky! It doesn't mean that God will magically wipe away those debts. It means that when you come to that place in prayer, Bible study, and commitment to accept, obey, and follow God's will for your life, then God will direct your every step in your financial situation.

As you take those God-given steps, you will experience hope long before that debt is paid! That hope will enable you to experience God's peace as you journey toward financial solvency.

Bible Verses to Overcome Lie #14

- "The steps of a good man are ordered by the Lord: and he delighteth in his way. Though he fall, he shall not be utterly cast down: for the Lord upholdeth him with his hand." Psalm 37:23,24 (KJV)

- "Order my steps in thy word: and let not any iniquity have dominion over me." Psalm 119:33 (KJV)

Related Scripture Passages

- The Book of Proverbs

Suggested Prayer Focus

1. Pray for forgiveness if you have not approached your finances in the way that God teaches in the Bible. Accept the fact that God has forgiven you and do not "beat yourself up" by recalling the financial mistakes you have made.

2. Commit to praying for a restored relationship with Jesus and righteous living more than for just financial recovery.

3. Ask God to show your heart that if you are willing to truly serve Jesus with every area of your life, the financial wisdom must and will follow.

4. Pray that you will recognize that worrying over finances instead of working under God's guidance to correct them is sin. That worry will hamper the close relationship you need with the Lord as you attempt to find solutions, comfort, and hope.

5. Pray to recognize that this will probably call for very long-term correction, possibly over a span of years.

6. Ask God to reveal to your heart a right relationship with Jesus. The peace you desire probably will come long before you see financial security. Pray for maturity in your financial decisions.

7. Pray to accept God's priorities on how you should spend whatever financial resources you have currently or will earn in the future.

8. Ask God to lead you to a wise Christian financial counselor.

Steps to Take to Overcome Lie #14

1. Look in a telephone directory or ask your pastor about a Christian financial counselor. Find one whose services are affordable for you, or even free. They do exist.

2. Contact the financial counselor immediately and make an appointment.

3. Keep that appointment and do not be embarrassed about your financial state. Millions, if not most, Americans are in debt. Overspending is a common problem in our nation. Jesus can empower you to overcome the tendency to spend beyond your means.

4. Follow any and all advice from your financial counselor as long as it is consistent with God's Word.

5. Until you can meet with a counselor, follow these common rules listed below:

6. Stop spending money that is already owed to existing bills.

7. Don't use credit cards for other than emergency situations. (An emergency would be a life-threatening situation or vehicle emergency repair for the vehicle you use to get to work.)

8. Don't sign any new contracts that obligate you financially until you can meet with your financial counselor.

9. Buy the bargain priced versions of the things you really need.

10. Don't dine out when you can eat less expensively at home.

11. Don't be tempted to write a check that may be returned for insufficient funds in order to meet a deadline. Make other payment arrangements with creditors. Returned checks carry heavy financial, and sometimes criminal, penalties.

12. Make financial decisions knowing that God expects you to pay your debt.

13. Recognize that God expects us to "tithe" (to give God the first ten-percent of whatever we earn). Discuss tithing with your financial counselor.

14. Make all financial decisions with God and all instruction from the Bible in mind. You cannot deceive, cheat, steal, ignore your debt, hold hatred for bill collectors, or ignore the tithe and have a right relationship with Jesus Christ.

15. You cannot have and maintain true hope until you have a right relationship with Jesus Christ.

Lie #15: *"I Have No Future Because of My Past!"*

This is the lie through which Satan attempts to distort three "time zones" in your life—the past, the present, and the future. If Satan can make us see only the negative results of our past, he can seemingly blind us to the opportunities of the present and attempt to conceal the hope of the future.

In all reality, he has no control over any of the three! Satan cannot change the past to make it as bad as he wants you to think it is. All he can do is infiltrate your thoughts with lies and illusions. Satan is not in control of the present, and he cannot foretell the future. Even if he could, he would lie about it. The Bible says:

There is no truth in him (John 8:44).

You have personally experienced Satan's lies, because he is the one who has made you feel that your previous choices have destroyed your future!

Why would Satan want to make your past seem worse than it really is, no matter what terrible things you have done? Because even in the most horrific situations, there are God-given ways to overcome them.

If Satan can make the things in your past seem worse than they are, he can make those things appear as if they can't be overcome. If Satan can defeat us mentally, then making us feel as though we are spiritually defeated is the next very easy step in making us ineffective for Christ and ineffective in our own lives.

The second way Satan deceives us is by continually pointing to the past. When we stare longingly or remorsefully at the past, we cannot see present opportunities or future possibilities. When we spend all of our time wallowing in the past, we have no time to search for present opportunities that could easily be seen if we were not blocked by a cloud of doubt and guilt.

When we allow ourselves to be tricked out of present opportunities, we start to panic about the future. Then we get so spiritually dizzy that we can't see how we could possibly have a decent future. We go through all of this simply because of a past we can't change!

Don't concentrate on the past. You cannot rewrite the past. You can, however, "write" the rest of your life story by surrendering your future to God and by living in a way that honors God! If you do that this very moment, you will be at a point in your life where your regrets will, through Christ, start to fade from your view.

As you begin to pray daily for God's will to be operative in your life, as you begin to diligently study the Bible for understanding, as you begin to walk hour-by-hour, day-by-day, and moment-by-moment with Jesus Christ, the future will increasingly and surprisingly reveal many opportunities for God to richly bless your life!

Do you think you can create an impossible situation for God? You cannot! That means nothing you have done in the past can destroy God's will for your future.

He knows the choices you have made; He knew long before you were born that you would make those wrong choices, Still, God has a wonderful will and plan for your future!

God's perfect will can take what Satan meant for bad and turn it into good! You can still be headed exactly where God now wants you to be in preparation for the future. Getting there may not be easy, but you will definitely be headed to a place where God wants you to be!

Maybe, like the apostle Paul, you are on your "road to Damascus," and today is the day you will truly begin to see the light of Jesus in your life. Paul had denied the Messiahship of Jesus, even unto the point of executing many who followed Jesus.

Paul had made many blasphemous, shameful and destructive choices in his past. He considered himself "chief" of sinners. Even after the anti-Jesus, deadly choices he made, God did not allow those choices to destroy God's future for him!

Following his conversion, the apostle Paul wrote in Philippians 3:13,14:

"Brethren, I count not myself to have apprehended: but this one thing I do, forgetting those things which are behind, and reaching forth unto those things which are before, I press toward the mark for the prize of the high calling of God in Christ Jesus."

By trusting God completely, obeying Him and going to Him with all your future choices, you will, through Jesus, overcome—but not undo—any and every wrong choice you have ever made!

Bible Verses to Overcome Lie #15

- "And we know that all things work together for good to them that love God, to them who are the called according to his purpose" Romans 8:28 (KJV).

- "Though I walk in the midst of trouble, thou wilt revive me: thou shalt stretch forth thine hand against the wrath of mine enemies, and thy right hand shall save me" Psalm 138:7 (KJV).

Related Scripture Passages

- John 8
- Ephesians 1-4
- Acts 6-10
- Galatians 3

Suggested Prayer Focus

1. Pray for forgiveness for any sinful choices of the past for which you have not sought forgiveness.

2. Pray for God to help you keep your mind from dwelling on past mistakes.

3. Pray for God to reveal to you present and future opportunities.

4. Forgive and ask God to forgive anyone who has wronged you.

5. Ask God to help you remember all good things and all good choices you made in the past.

6. Pray for God to allow lessons that you learned in your past choices to stay with you, without being bothered by the painful memories or the feelings they once caused.

7. Pray for God to enable you to overcome your past for His glory, and for the honor and glory of Jesus Christ.

8. Devote your life now and your future to the complete lordship of Jesus. Pray for God's will to prevail in your future.

Steps to Take to Overcome Lie #15

1. Remove any items from your environment that serve as constant reminders of bad choices you made previously.

2. Avoid conversations that dwell on the past. Even conversations about past "glory days" may eventually end up with thoughts about bad previous choices.

3. Do not try to live up to childhood dreams that were not based on mature reality.

4. Do not entertain thoughts that begin with, "If only I had ..."

5. Begin to research realistic options that exist for you currently.

6. Do not compare current options to what might have been if your past had been different.

7. Pray hard to recognize, believe, accept, and act upon the truth that you are a new creature in Christ Jesus.

8. Based on where you are right now in life, make new dreams, goals, and plans for the future. What do you think God would have you doing in five years? In ten years?

9. Make yearly, monthly, weekly, and daily goals that will help you accomplish those dreams.

10. Begin to fill your mind with stories of Christians who also made mistakes but who overcame them.

11. Make new friends and engage in new Christian activities that do not lend themselves to similar choices you made in the past.

12. Stay away from situations that challenge your weakest decision-making areas. Avoid temptation so that you won't yield to it.

13. Do not accept "giving up" as an option for your life.

14. Pray continually for strength to see your way through until better days arrive.

15. Remember that if you dwell on your past, you are letting Satan destroy your present, and in the future, you will regret what you are losing today also.

16. Commit each day, one day at a time, to living for God and trusting Him. Eventually, you will have years of good choices between you and any choices you thought had destroyed your future. Your future will then be based on years of living for God.

Lie #16: "I'll Never Have a Job that I Enjoy!"

What's that you say? "God can never get me a job that I enjoy?" When you believe that you will never get a job you like, doesn't that imply, "Even God can never get me a job that I enjoy"?

If you admit that it is possible for God to get you a job or career you enjoy, that means "never" is not true! So if you are unemployed or unfulfilled in the work you now do, why have you lost hope about getting another job?

If you truly believe that you can never get a job you will enjoy, it means you must be declaring one of two things:

1. God cannot do it.

2. God will not do it.

Which one are you declaring?

You know in your heart that God can do anything, so you can't possibly believe that, "Even God cannot do it."

That means you are probably thinking, "God will not do it." Did God tell you this personally, or do you somehow believe that you now have the power to know all that God will or will not do in the future? You cannot know all that God will do, but you can know some of what God's Word promises He will do. You also can know what the Bible teaches is best for you to do regarding work!

First, let's look at what God promises He will do that can help you find a job or career you enjoy. Let's start with a passage from the Bible that addresses this issue in many ways. Psalm 37:3-5 states:

> Trust in the LORD, and do good; so shalt thou dwell in the land, and verily thou shalt be fed. Delight thyself also in the LORD; and he shall give thee the desires of thine heart. Commit thy way unto the LORD; trust also in him; and he shall bring it to pass.

God promises us that if we trust in Him, delight in Him, and commit our way to Him, He will give us the desires of our heart and bring it to pass! Does that mean that if you do all of those things He will give you the current desires of your heart? That depends on what your heart desires. But that's the way many people interpret this passage, but let's look at the faulty reasoning in that interpretation.

Using that interpretation, would that mean if your desire is to be the manager of a bar or topless club, that if you commit your way to the Lord, He will grant you that desire of your heart? Is that what this scripture means? Absolutely not!

What this passage promises is that if you trust in the Lord, if you delight in Him, and if you commit your way to Him, then He will give you new desires of the heart, new desires that are aligned with His will. Then, if you commit your way to Him, He promises to fulfill the new desires He will give you. He shall bring them to pass, if you trust Him. (This passage mentions trust twice, so it must be important!)

No matter how you assess it, if you do what is called for in Psalm 37, you will eventually obtain a job you enjoy! That's just one of the promises God makes for His part in your getting a job that is according to the desires of your heart.

What is your part in someday finding a fulfilling career, or maybe even love. First, you must answer to that promise by trusting in the Lord. While you are still saying, "I can/will never _____" you are really saying, "God can/will never _____." That's definitely not trust!

Second, you must delight in Him. You must put more delight in Him than in your job. Third, you must commit your way to Him. Your way might not include the job you are dreaming of now. God will keep His promise for His part; you just have to do your part!

Another verse of Scripture that addresses "your part" is in Ecclesiastes 2:24:

A man can do nothing better than to eat and drink and find satisfaction in his work. This too, I see, is from the hand of God (NIV).

You must make your soul enjoy good in your labor. If you do that—and you can through God—you will always have a job you like, no matter where you work, no matter what you do!

Bible Verses to Overcome Lie #16

- Serve wholeheartedly, as if you were serving the Lord, not men. Ephesians 6:7 (NIV)

- There is nothing better for a man, than that he should eat and drink, and that he should make his soul enjoy good in his labour. This also I saw, that it was from the hand of God....And also that every man should eat and drink, and enjoy the good of all his labour, it is the gift of God. Ecclesiastes 2:24;3:13

Related Scripture Passages

- The Book of Ecclesiastes

Suggested Prayer Focus

1. Pray to understand what God says, through His Word, about respecting one type of honest work more than another.

2. Pray to know and accept God's will for your life regarding the type of job or career He has in store for you.

3. Pray to distinguish clearly between your desires and expectations, others' expectations for you,

and God's will for you. (Keep in mind that often the three do not match.)

4. Pray for peace and a sense of fulfillment concerning whatever work you do currently until you find out what God would have you to do. Also pray to be made aware of when you must keep seeking for the job or career that will give you true fulfillment.

5. Pray for perseverance as you search for a more fulfilling job or career.

6. Ask God to help you enjoy whatever work assignment you receive from Him. Pray to be a witness in your workplace.

7. Pray for the resources you need to develop the skills, knowledge, and motivation to do your job to the best of your ability.

Steps to Take to Overcome Lie #16

1. Stop dwelling on thoughts about things you hate about your current line of work.

2. Especially stop dwelling on things you cannot change.

3. Stop any complaining about getting better working conditions, better treatment, or more perks from your employer.

4. Start concentrating on ways you can contribute to improving conditions at work, treating peo-

ple better, and being more profitable for your present employer. Develop a better attitude about your current employment situation.

5. Do not expect people to "pat you on the back," to help you in your efforts, or even to notice your efforts. Do your very best or put forth an extra effort because that's what Jesus would do, and expects you to do, not to be praised.

6. Commit to being the best employee you can in any position where you work. Always be honest and fair in your business dealings. When an opportunity presents itself at your current job, you will be a better candidate for that position when you work with honesty and fairness.

7. Do not pout or complain to God, your employer, your friends, or in private when you do not get what you want. Trust God to provide the desires of your heart.

8. Make sure you know and understand your employer's needs, desires and wishes concerning your work and strive to meet or exceed them when it does not conflict with Scripture.

9. Pray and ask God to direct you to the job you believe He would have you to do. Research the qualifications for that job. Train and prepare for those qualifications if you do not have them already.

10. Be prepared to "work your way up" to the position you desire—kind of like "playing the farm league" until you get to the major league. Ignore unrealistic hopes.

11. Do not dream of another job while you are at work. Keep all your desires, thoughts, and efforts to change positions off of your present employer's time-card. Remember, you can't give 100 percent to your employer when you are dreaming of another job. It's not what God would have you to do.

12. Never look down on anyone, including yourself, because of the type of work that person does or because they lack status on the job.

13. Do all your work as unto the Lord. Give your employer an honest day's work.

Lie #17:
"Only Weak People Need Help!"

This is the cry of the proud and the haughty. This is also the lie of the proud and the haughty. People usually only use this untruth to look down on someone else. If they use this statement toward others, it is generally because of the sin of pride, counting their personal achievements to their own glory, not God's.

Sometimes we use this lie to look down on ourselves as failures or underachievers when we do not live up to our own unrealistic expectations of what we should be capable of doing.

Either way, it is a lie. Either way, it does not line up with the Truth and examples in the Bible. You don't have to go any further than the first man in the Bible to see the truth about humankind needing help!

The Bible teaches that God made Adam in His own image. While Adam was still sinless, he had to represent the most perfect form of human possible (outside of Jesus Christ). Even deterioration and aging had not entered into humankind before sin. Adam was as perfect in every way.

What was God's view of man and the goodness of help? According to Genesis 2:18:

> The LORD God said, "It is not good for the man to be alone. I will make a helper suitable for him."

Adam—who, at that time, was a perfect physical human specimen, without the effects of aging and deterioration, whole, without sickness, sinless, without error or mistake yet made—was given a helper with God's blessings and within God's design for humankind!

The word "help" is mentioned at least 126 times in the Bible. Solomon, the wisest man who ever lived, needed help at one point in his life. The mighty King David specifically requested help from God in the Psalms. Throughout Scripture, we see mighty men and women, kings and soldiers, armies, cities, tribes, families, even churches needing and receiving help, sometimes directly from God, sometimes from God through men, women, and children.

Mighty men of valor, kings, and statesmen often sought the counsel, or help, of wise men, friends, mothers, brothers, sisters, and fathers. In times of trouble, famine, and even in times of blessing and harvest, many persons in the Bible sought help. Many were offered help by God, some even before they could ask for it.

The very design of the order of nature and the heavens suggests that help is proper, necessary, required, expected, and God-ordained.

The earth, without the aid of the sun, would freeze in bitter cold and darkness. Without the moon, the earth would have no tides to move the seas. The moon, without the pull of earth's gravity, would not hang in the proper position in space to help the earth or light its night.

God said that man needed the help of woman, woman needs man, children are God's gifts to parents and parents help children to become adults. Plants need the help of animals (exchanging molecules necessary for survival), animals need the nourishment and oxygen provided by plants.

God's chosen people would have failed in many battles without God's help. The wise men who sought out the Christ-child, Jesus, the King of Kings needed the help of the star. Even Solomon, the wisest man to ever live, made some foolish decisions when he sought to act without the help of God-given wisdom!

Knowing that many people would need help so many times throughout history, God saw fit to allow armies of angels, under His divine guidance, to help humankind. All of creation allows for help, not only among the weak!

The ultimate example of someone who received help is the Lord, Jesus Christ, Himself. He, being the very Son of God, God incarnate, while a man on earth considered it no shame to allow His disciples to help Him spread the Gospel message. Even upon His return to earth as King of Kings and Lord of Lords, He will allow the help of angels and the perfected saints in the Battle of Armageddon, the greatest battle of all time!

Help is not just for the weak, it is in the very order of all creation, God's creation!

Bible Verses to Overcome Lie #17

- "And the LORD shall help them, and deliver them: he shall deliver them from the wicked, and save them, because they trust in him ..." Psalm 37:40 (KJV)

- "Let us therefore come boldly unto the throne of grace, that we may obtain mercy, and find grace to help in time of need." Hebrews 4:16 (KJV)

Related Scripture Passages

- Matthew 6:9-34
- Luke 6:13-16
- Genesis 2:19-24
- Acts 12:29

Suggested Prayer Focus

1. Pray to accept that humankind was designed to receive help.

2. Pray, confess, and ask forgiveness for the sin of pride. Pride is what makes us feel badly for accepting help. Pride says, "I'm too good for that. Other people need help, but not me."

3. Pray to understand that there is no godly reason to deny God-given help offered through others.

4. Pray for ways to receive help that will bless the person helping you.

5. Pray to realize that just allowing someone to help you is a blessing because it enables them to serve God by helping you and others.

6. Pray for the maturity to be gracious and grateful toward those who offer help.

7. Pray not to be envious of those who help you or even of others who do not need help.

8. Pray to maintain a good relationship with the Lord that is not hindered by current needs, desires, wishes, or hardships.

9. Pray to recognize that all help is from God. Thank Him for all help that He sends to you. Thank and praise Jesus for being with you in your need.

Steps to Take to Overcome Lie #17

1. Try to remember the times you have helped others. Recall the way you felt about helping those persons. Did you think of them as being weak simply because they needed help?

2. Try to remember the times when someone you recognized as strong, as a leader, or even as an average person, asked you or anyone for help. How did you respond to their request?

3. Read stories about people you respect. Make a mental note of any time they accepted help in any way from anyone.

4. Watch events that occur during your time of need. Notice and make a mental note of every action that requires more than one person.

5. Make a list of every organization you know of that has as its mission to help people. List as many national and international help organizations as you can.

6. Observe that those organizations exist specifically because many people need help at different times in their lives.

7. Note that many people who seek the help of those organizations have at times been ultra-successful in the eyes of society.

8. It should be understood that no one could rightfully call those people weak, and that many of those people recover because of help they have received, then go on to be successful leaders again.

9. Instead of concentrating on being ashamed of needing and accepting help, think about ways you can return the favor by helping others when you come to a stronger point in your life. Help others in ways you can, even if you still need help yourself.

10. Accept all help that comes from the Lord. Do your part to recover.

11. Witness to others while accepting help. Tell them that you hope someday the Lord will allow you to help them in their time of need.

12. Try to use every opportunity to lead those who are helping you to salvation through Christ.

13. When you are at the point where you truly have faith that God will recover you from your situation, tell your story as a witness to those who are helping you. Ask if they will let you pray for them.

Lie #18: *"There's No More Good in the World!"*

This probably should be called "the lie that sells." Because of our natural sinful nature, we tend to be drawn to sin, tragedy, danger, scary things, lustful things, earthly riches, tempting things, and many various ungodly things.

That's why the secular media tend to produce, sell, distribute, and broadcast programs, shows, books, magazines, internet sites, advertising and more that do not show good things. Bad sells easily; good is a hard sell.

Regardless of the reason, it is just a complete lie that there is no more good in the world. It is impossible. As long as Christians dwell on the earth, there will be good in the world. As long as there are believers in this world, there will always be good because Jesus dwells in the hearts and lives of those who believe in Him. The Bible also teaches that until Jesus returns, the Holy Spirit, the Comforter, will remain here for Christians.

There are Christians still on earth. As a matter of fact, the film "Jesus" reports there are over one billion followers of Christ! That's a lot of good in the world!

With Jesus dwelling in the hearts of over one billion followers, by virtue of sheer statistics, at any given time, there are millions of good things still happening all over the world.

At any given moment, statistically speaking, there must be millions of people praying all over the world. Some of them are praying in various sized groups, while others are praying individually. Many are literally praying for your needs—whether for your salvation, your physical needs, your spiritual needs, psychological needs, financial needs, moral encouragement—whatever help you really need at this very moment.

With the number of people each of us encounter in life, there is a great possibility that some of the people you know are praying for you by name right now! If you have given your life to Jesus, you yourself can pray directly to God for your needs, right now!

At any given moment, there are millions of people around the world witnessing for Christ, and millions of people sharing the good news of Jesus Christ! At any given moment, millions of people around the world are reading the Bible, God's precious love story for humanity.

At any given moment, millions of people are meeting, two or more at a time, learning about and discussing the truths of the Bible. They can impact their own lives as well as the lives of those they will come in contact with, including you.

Even in the communist countries of the world, house churches meet in secret and believers spread the Gospel. Even under threat of persecution, God continues to bless them with peace and Christian

you believe there is no more good in the world. Avoid such programs.

11. Seek and join organizations that do good things. Start with church! Attend church regularly.

12. Organize and lead other people to do good things.

13. Do not participate in anything that will make someone else believe there is no more good in the world.

14. Greatly increase your prayer life, Bible study, and church attendance. In doing so, you should no longer believe that all good has left our world.

Lie #19:
"My Life Can Be Just Like in the Movies!"

If you're old enough and educated enough to read and comprehend these words, you've already proven that your life cannot be like a movie. How so? Well for starters, if your life was only as long as a movie, your entire life would be over in about two hours! You wouldn't have even had time to learn to read this or anything else!

That's the first thing that makes it impossible for our lives to be like the movies. Any movie lifestyle you have ever envied, dreamed of, or wanted to live is based on two hours of drama. If that drama was based on a true story, you only saw two hours out of a story that actually stretched over a span of days, weeks, months, years, or even centuries. If there was any truth in the production you envied, it is generally embellished upon or exaggerated to make it more interesting. Even truth that is stretched is no longer the truth!

This is not to say that all writers or producers are intentionally deceiving you, though some are. It means that the story lines are intentionally changed, filled in, cut down, changed around, purposefully skewed, edited, enhanced, or hyped up in order to bring more excitement to the viewer. When we ourselves begin to believe that our lives can be like that, we are the ones lying to ourselves!

Once we believe that our lives can be like those in the movies, we start to become jealous and envious of the things, events, actions, people, and story lines as we compare them to our own lives. We begin to feel many unhealthy emotions such as frustration, doubt, anger, fear, anxiety, confusion, depression, and more.

It is bad enough when the story has a little truth in it, but it is often even more unrealistic and damaging when it is complete fiction. This does not mean that fiction is bad by virtue of being fiction.

The point is that any life that is fit neatly into a two-hour time frame cannot represent the whole picture. For example, to cut an entire lifetime down to two hours, all the boring, mundane, and routine events of life that would literally add up to years of film must be removed. Even our greatest heroes and heroines are known mostly for a few glorious moments or events out of an entire lifetime. When we watch movies about astronauts, war heroes, athletes, or other positive role models, we watch a mere fraction of a lifetime of hard work, sacrifice, and routine, mundane actions that they endured in order to achieve their moment of glory.

Often times, even minutes of glory on film were really seconds of glory shown in slow motion or over and over again from alternating camera angles. Those few minutes are then enhanced with music sound tracks and special effects that were nowhere around during the real event!

Many times it is one single event out of a lifetime that makes us idolize the lives of our positive role models. It is good when positive role models in positive situations can inspire us to achieve great things in life. But just think what happens when people allow themselves and their desires to be purposefully distorted via negative role models and negative situations.

Movies that glorify criminals, crime, evil characters, immorality, and sinful plots distort the situations and characters almost to the point of being completely opposite of real life. Criminals with guns are often portrayed as brave, macho leaders, when in reality they generally are so afraid of failure that they can't compete in normal society without a weapon.

Those movies also show minutes or seconds of "glory" that really aren't glory at all. They don't show the years of physical, mental, spiritual, moral, and psychological anguish those men and women suffered because of their crimes, sins, and evil deeds. Movies often don't show the dysfunctional homes that served as the catalyst to the questionable lifestyles.

Those movies do not show years of prison time and the cruelties of rape, abuse, loneliness, filthiness, manipulation and shame, injuries, or even deaths that prison life brings. They don't show the shame, depression, and anxiety of life that running from the law brings.

Life is not a movie and we should not try to live our lives as though it is. We need to be grateful for the real lives God has given us, and spend our lives with the real Savior, Jesus Christ, whose love makes real life, even a difficult life, better than any movie could ever be!

Bible Verses to Overcome Lie #19

- "For all that is in the world, the lust of the flesh, and the lust of the eyes, and the pride of life, is not of the Father, but is of the world." 1 John 2:16 (KJV)

- "For wrath killeth the foolish man, and envy slayeth the silly one." Job 5:2 (KJV)

Related Scripture Passages

- James 3:14-18
- Matthew 6:22,23
- Romans 13
- Proverb 14:30

Suggested Prayer Focus

1. Pray for the deception of fantasy and drama to be removed from your heart and mind as your perception of reality.

2. Pray for wisdom to distinguish between the real and truthful parts of movies and the exaggerated hype.

3. Pray for the void—the root cause of a desire to have an unrealistic fantasy life—to be filled with Jesus' love.

4. Pray for a mature understanding of life.

5. Pray for a more biblical perception of what your life, and life in general, should be.

6. Pray to recognize right from wrong as in movies that may cause you to compromise your values in real life.

7. Pray to recognize and understand the real life dangers, tragedies, and heartaches that come from attempting to imitate cinema fantasy.

8. Pray to recognize that real life friendships, relationships, love, and marriage cannot be "just like the movies."

9. Pray to find the true God-given excitement, rewards, and hope that we have in the real world, even in bad situations.

Steps to Take to Overcome Lie #19

1. For each movie star or other media personality that you would like to be like, next to each name, list why you want to be like them.

2. Find out the real life requirements (if there are any) to attain those things, the real life costs, and the real life amount of time and effort it takes to accomplish those things in the movies.

3. If you still want to accomplish those things, you must approach your goal with real life standards to meet.

4. Of the things you want to try, first compare them with what the Bible teaches is right or wrong. If the Bible teaches those things are wrong, do not even attempt to accomplish them. Pray for the strength to let go of ungodly desires.

5. If you have any remaining things that the Bible does not teach against specifically, compare those things to what you know beyond a shadow of a doubt is God's will for your life.

6. If you don't know God's will for your life, begin a steady campaign of prayer to discover His will for you.

7. Present the list of goals you got from the movie to your pastor, your Sunday school teacher, or to a wise Christian counselor.

8. If those ideas are accepted as realistic and Christian by the person with wise counsel, continue to pray about ways to reach those goals. Then diligently seek real life expectations to set about doing those things.

9. After all of that advice, there should not be too many things left from the movies that you would want to do. If there are any, at least you

will have a more realistic, more scriptural approach to accomplishing those goals.

10. If any of your movie "heroes" or "heroines" are criminals, evil characters, or non-Christian people, you should consider receiving personal, informal counseling from your pastor.

11. Ask your pastor to explain what it truly means to be a Christian and how that fits or doesn't fit with the movie lifestyles you envy.

Lie #20:
"There's No Hope for My Family!"

If you are thinking this about your family, you need to know that there is God-given hope for all families! Nothing in this world can erase the hope that is God-given through Jesus Christ for the family unit—that includes your family.

This does not mean that your family is supposed to be perfect. Families have problems and individual family members do not always treat other family members with love and fairness.

Some families carry with them bad reputations. They are known for having generations of ne'er-do-wells, convicts, thieves or liars. Even if there are people in your family who have done terrible things, remember that everyone in your family has the opportunity to accept or deny the lordship of Jesus through confession, repentance and salvation in faith through Christ.

Anyone who does that is then entitled to all of the promises of the Bible that apply to all Christians! Everyone in your family who accepts Jesus as Lord can do so. Everyone in your family who has already accepted Jesus Christ as Lord and Savior can pray to God directly! No one in the world can stop that!

Any person in your family who is a Christian can claim every promise of the Bible that applies directly to our lives on earth. Jesus died for everyone! God created the family unit for our own nurture, growth, survival and development. God loves all families! God's Word addresses the importance of the family! Jesus loves your family!

How does all that apply to our lives here on earth? The Bible is God's Word. It is complete truth! Any verse that applies to humanity in general applies to your family. Any verse that applies to every family also applies to you and your family.

That means members of your family, like all others, have fallen in sin. Individuals who are members of your family, like all others, can be forgiven by God's family through believing in Jesus Christ, repenting of sin, and accepting Jesus as Lord. When they do that, they rightfully claim all of the promises of their Father in heaven, God. All these promises are true because they are God's promises, and the Bible is never wrong!

All of God's promises can be proven because history itself gives clear examples of the fulfillment of His promises. No matter what members of your family have done, there are individuals who have lived lives that show that the promises of God apply to everyone in family.

Every family has a last name by which they are identified. Some even have a crest or a coat of arms to identify themselves. Some families have a reputation for being godly, upstanding, and honorable. Other families are notorious for being troublemakers or uncivil, rude, or disrespectful. No matter what reputation your family has, there have been some members of your family who have denied the lordship of Jesus Christ and the truth of the Bible. Their lives have been lived in ways that did not honor God or your family. Eventually, those individuals died or will die denying Christ and are now or will someday be in hell forever. That is true of every family!

There have been many members of your family who have accepted Jesus Christ as Lord, learned and lived the truth of the Bible, even through tragedy and strife, and lived their lives in ways that honored God and your family. Eventually, those individuals died or will die to their earthly bodies, but will live in heaven forever in sinless perfection with the Father and the Son! That is true of every family!

God has blessed many persons of every family in ways that can never be measured by earthly standards. But even by earthly standards, those in your family who have committed their lives to Christ have been blessed and honored.

No matter what family you were born into, there are those in your family who have been kings, queens, doctors, lawyers, authors, poets, inventors, scientists, war heroes, engineers, astronauts, models, sports heroes, preachers, evangelists, nurses, soldiers, teachers, and every other sort of occupation.

There have been all sorts of families and their members—rich and poor, famous and infamous, educated and uneducated, employed and unemployed, disabled and perfect physical specimens, slave and free, who have been blessed by God in all of the truth and promises of the Bible.

As long as the human family is on earth, Christians in your beautiful, God-designed family can claim all of the rights and responsibilities that come from following Jesus Christ.

What hope do you need concerning your family that is aligned with Scripture? Live completely for Christ as He taught. If you do, you will receive God's promises and the offer of His will for your life! Encourage others in your family to live for Him, too. Witness to family members who don't know Him. People can be very effective witnessing to persons in their own family. Spread hope to your family by telling them about Jesus.

Bible Verses to Overcome Lie #20

- While Jesus was still talking to the crowd, his mother and brothers stood outside, wanting to speak to him. Someone told him, "Your mother and brothers are standing outside, wanting to speak to you." He replied to him, "Who is my mother, and who are my brothers?" Pointing to his disciples, he said, "Here are my mother and my brothers. For whoever does the will of my Father in heaven is my brother and sister and mother." Matt. 12:46-50 (NIV)

- So God created man in his own image, in the image of God he created him; male and female he created them. God blessed them and said to them, "Be fruitful and increase in number." Genesis 1:27-28 (NIV)

Related Scripture Passages

- 1 Chronicles 16:43
- Acts 16:33-34
- Galatians 6:10
- Psalm 68:6

Suggested Prayer Focus

1. Pray to understand that because God gave His own Son's life for you and everyone in your family, you have the greatest hope of all—true hope through Jesus Christ!

2. Praise God for the incomprehensible wisdom to create your family for you and the rest of your family to enjoy.

3. Praise God for blessing you to be a member of the best possible family for you to meet His will for you in life.

4. Praise God for all the ways He has blessed your family and you as a member of that family.

5. Praise God for all the ways He has used your family to bless each other.

6. Praise God for loving your family so much that He let His Son die for your family and rise to live again for your family as Savior.

7. Praise Jesus for sacrificing His life and His blood so that as many from your family as will follow Him can be by His side for eternity.

8. Praise God for all of the members of your family who have already seen and are living the promise of eternity in heaven.

9. Forgive those family members who have hurt you or other family members. If you cannot yet bring yourself to forgive them, pray for the desire to forgive.

10. Pray for family members with addictions, sinful habits, or who have other lingering problems that affect the entire family.

Steps to Take to Overcome Lie #20

1. Do not engage in any conversations that imply there is no hope for your family.

2. Never believe or make comments that would make other members of your family feel that there is no hope. Learn the Bible's messages of truth and hope for your family, so you can share it with them.

3. Talk to the person in your family or closest friend of the same family who has been a

Christian longer than any other you know. Ask them what hope they see for your family.

4. Do some research to find out about your family history. Try to find out about persons who can be positive role models for the present generations.

5. Talk to the eldest member of your family. Ask them to share positive stories about your family with you and the younger generations.

6. Take the time to learn about members of your family about whom you don't know much. Learn about their impressions and visions of hope for your family.

7. Read stories about famous Christian leaders and evangelists of your family. Learn about their hope for your family.

9. Pick any area of life that interests you. Find out if someone in your family has accomplished great things in that area. Find out if there are any areas of specialty or gifts that are common among members of your family (such as writing, singing, art, woodworking, etc.).

10. Be one of the people in your family who builds hope for the future of your family through the power of Jesus Christ.

11. Find out about the religious background of your family. Search for a church that provides activities and interests for the entire family (if you don't have one now.)

Lie #21:
"Life Should Always Be Fun and Exciting!"

This statement is not true according to Scripture! It's not surprising that there are those in the world who would have us believe that life should always be fun and exciting. You probably know many Christians who also teach or believe the same thing. Either way, it is not true!

There is nothing in the Bible to suggest that every moment of life will be fun or exciting. As a matter of fact, there are thousands of situations in the Bible where the lives of God's people, in both the Old and New Testaments, were neither fun nor exciting.

But isn't it okay to teach that life with Jesus is fun and exciting? It is scriptural to teach, at times, that life with Jesus is fun and exciting; but it doesn't mean that every moment, or even every day, is fun or exciting!

How could anyone dare say such a thing? Just look at the Scriptures. Look at the very life of Jesus! At the moment that Jesus learned of His friend Lazarus' death, when Jesus wept, do you think He wept because life was fun at that moment? Obviously not!

When Jesus was being run out of the different towns, mocked, cursed, spit on, beaten, whipped, crowned with thorns, and had nails driven into His hands and feet to be crucified, do you think His life was fun and exciting then? It was not!

Why then, would people say that life, even with Jesus, is always fun and exciting? Basically, because they mean well, but have not thought about what the Scriptures really teach. The Bible says in the Book of Ecclesiastes that:

There is a time for everything, and a season for every activity under heaven: a time to be born and a time to die, a time to plant and a time to uproot,a time to kill and a time to heal, a time to tear down and a time to build, a time to weep and a time to laugh, a time to mourn and a time to dance, a time to scatter stones and a time to gather them, a time to embrace and a time to refrain, a time to search and a time to give up, a time to keep and a time to throw away, a time to tear and a time to mend, a time to be silent and a time to speak, a time to love and a time to hate, a time for war and a time for peace.

Do these sound like fun times? No, they do not, and they are not supposed to. That's where we find difficulty with the teachings that suggest all of our times with Jesus will be fun and exciting. This position does not agree with the Scripture, it does not agree with the truth, and it is a hope-destroying lie that sets people up for depression, loss of faith in God, and loss of a close walk with Jesus.

Any time people find they have placed their hope in a lie, whether it sounds nice or not, they will lose hope when that lie does not come true.

Instead, the Bible teaches us that life with Jesus will give us joy that is not earth-bound. Life with Jesus will give us more strength, peace, and hope to make it through the hard times and persecutions that are promised to Christians. It teaches us that, through Christ, we will overcome! That is true hope, through Christ!

Conversely, some people in our world would have us to think that life without Christ is always fun and exciting and that life with Christ is never fun or exciting. Sometimes when their Christian friends lose hope, they say, "I thought your life with Christ was always supposed to be wonderful. I guess Jesus failed." Those are all lies about fun and excitement as well.

Life without Christ is not always "fun," as the world would have you think. Do you think hangovers, drug addiction, unwanted pregnancies, abortion, divorce, sexually transmitted diseases, infidelity, jail time, prison, debt, death by DUI, death by capital punishment, or eternity in hell are fun? Those are all real experiences of life in opposition to the teachings of Christ.

It is also a lie to think that Christians never have any fun. There are many things you can do as a Christian that are fun and exciting. It is very exciting to share Christian love with those in need. It is fun to enjoy family times that honor God. It is exciting to see the life-changing power of the Gospel of Jesus Christ at work in those around you. It is extremely exciting to know that God hears the prayers of those who love and follow Christ. It is unsurpassably rewarding to know that when you die, you will spend eternity in heaven instead of hell! That is the ultimate expression of excitement!

There is time for fun and excitement in the Christian life, but if we remember that sad times and hard times are equally scriptural, we are less likely to dive into depression every time we must work, weep, mourn, or suffer! Fun, like all else, is best kept within a godly balance.

Remember, every human being has hard times between the fun times, but only Christians have Jesus as their personal Savior during those difficult times!

Bible Verses to Overcome Lie #21

- "As a dog returneth to his vomit, so a fool returneth to his folly." Proverb 26:11 (KJV)

- "They that sow in tears shall reap in joy." Psalm 126:5 (KJV)

Related Scripture Passages

- Ecclesiastes 3:1-8
- John 11:1-45
- Galatians 5:19-21
- Matthew 25

Suggested Prayer Focus

1. Pray for God to reveal to your heart the truth about "fun" and "excitement." Fun and excitement are of God when they come through godly living; but godly living is not always fun and exciting.

2. Pray for God to open your eyes and reveal to your heart the truth that the worldly way is not as fun as it seems.

3. Pray for God to reveal the things in your life that are acceptable fun to Him and the things that are not.

4. Pray not to feel guilty about having fun and excitement when God grants it within His will.

5. Pray to have wisdom about how to share a godly perspective about what life should really be like according to Scripture.

6. Pray to know that a life with no fun or excitement is equally unscriptural and unbalanced, and a sign that something is not right in your relationship with Jesus.

7. Pray to realize that truly good times are gifts from the Lord.

8. Pray to accept truly that bad or sorrowful times cannot come without God's permission. When they happen, there is always a reason. Some reasons He will reveal. Some He won't.

9. Pray to realize that Jesus is with you in both good times and bad.

Steps to Take to Overcome Lie #21

1. For any fun event, item, or situation you strongly envy, make a list of all the bad things you can think of that come along with each situation. Be honest and think as hard as you can. Keep the list to work on as long as you are longing for any certain item, event, or situation that is now missing from your life.

2. For any event, item, or situation you believe is simply one of the burdens of being a Christian, make a list of all the good things that result from those burdens or "non-fun" times.

3. Do not try to convince yourself that everything in the Christian life is "fun." You are trying to see that everything has a purpose and some good comes from everything God would have us do or endure.

4. Make a list of anything you think is bad or hard that results from living a Christian life. Be honest in your assessment.

5. Make a list of anything you think is bad or hard that results from living a worldly life. Be honest in your assessment.

6. Make a list of anything you believe is good or rewarding that comes from living a Christian life.

7. Make a list of anything you think is good or rewarding that comes from living a worldly life.

8. Compare the lists and pick the one you believe you would rather live.

9. When you have done that, you will have chosen between following Jesus for all that it means and rejecting Jesus for all that it means.

10. If you do not choose the worldly way, your main priority in life should be to seek a proper relationship with Jesus as Lord. Nothing else matters until you do.

11. If you choose the Christian life, you should ask God for forgiveness for envying the worldly life. Then ask God to restore your close relationship with Jesus, change your focus, and remove envy from your heart.

12. Pray and seek to find excitement and fun in ways that will please the Lord. Have fun when it's godly, but don't when it's not.

Lie #22:
"Everyone Has the Same Opportunities."

This is one lie which might be wonderful if it were true, but we will never know! It is simply impossible. It is a worthy goal, and it is great for society to attempt to give as many opportunities as possible to everyone, but it is physically impossible for everyone to have all of the same opportunities.

Consider this for a simple illustration: Suppose that someone was trying to make it possible for every person in the world to fly to Hawaii for a vacation. Even if the person could reserve the same accommodations for most people, it would be impossible to make all arrangements that are completely equal and the same.

Even if everyone in the world could go to Hawaii, they all could not go on the same flight. A giant airplane could not take off from every airport in the world at the same time. Even if the airlines could be coordinated to do this, everyone would not have a window seat. If they could, would they all be the first seat, last seat, or middle seat?

Who would get their peanuts first, or would every person get peanuts served simultaneously by their own personal flight attendant? (What about those who don't like peanuts?)

Even if all that were possible, could everyone from the flight to Hawaii stay in the best room on the same day? No. Do you see how the more people involved, the more impossible it becomes to give everyone the same opportunity?

It may seem ridiculous to carry such a simple example to such extremes. But as simple as this example is, just think how impossible it becomes for everyone to have the same opportunities in complex situations when there are even fewer resources, or when the number of people considered reaches into the billions!

To say that all people should have as many opportunities possible is a worthy goal. To say all people do have or can have the same opportunities is a lie, however. Let's look at a more serious example. Children in our country are taught that they all have the same opportunity to grow up and be senators, or even president.

Even if every child lived the perfect life to fulfill that aspiration, there are only two senators from every state at any given time. It is virtually impossible for all members of a single graduating class to all be elected senators in one life-time during their adult years.

Claiming that everyone has, or can ever have, the same opportunities destroys hope in two ways. First, it gives those in positions to create opportunities little motivation to do so. They pacify themselves by believing that since everyone has equal opportunity available to them; therefore, they are under no obligation to extend themselves to help those who are disadvantaged. Mentoring programs like Big Brothers and Sisters, InRoads and others would not be needed if everyone was born with the same opportunities.

By not recognizing the truth about the lack of opportunities for some, even fewer opportunities will then be created. More people will have fewer opportunities; therefore, those people will have less hope.

Second, those who do not have a number of opportunities available to them, loss of hope can come in two ways:

1. Believing that everyone is supposed to have the same opportunity means that if they do not get those opportunities, they are set up for depression, self-pity, loss of self-responsibility, and eventually, loss of hope.

2. Believing that everyone is supposed to have the same opportunity means that if they do not accomplish a particular thing, they can judge themselves, or believe the judgment by others of themselves as failures and lose hope.

The Bible teaches that we are all given various gifts and abilities in varying measure, according to God's purpose and God's will. The Bible teaches that we are judged according to what we do with our God-given measures of ability, not by the opportunities human beings give us.

The Bible teaches in 1 Samuel 2:7-8:

The LORD maketh poor, and maketh rich: he bringeth low, and lifteth up.

This means God ultimately gives opportunities as He sees fit, and we do not have to turn to man for opportunity, but to God.

The Bible also reveals in Jeremiah 17:10 (KJV):

I, the LORD, search the heart, I try the reins, even to give every man according to his ways, and according to the fruit of his doings.

This, too, gives us hope, because although we cannot have every opportunity in this world, we can receive blessings of opportunity according to the fruit of our doings!

Make all of the fruit of your doings fruit unto the Lord and be given accordingly—that is a God-given opportunity and promise!

Bible Verses to Overcome Lie #22

- "Humble yourselves in the sight of the Lord, and he shall lift you up." James 4:10 (KJV)

- "The wise shall inherit glory: but shame shall be the promotion of fools." Proverb 3:35 (KJV)

Related Scripture Passages

- Genesis 27-31
- Luke 16:19-21
- John 5:1-8
- Exodus 5:1-19

Suggested Prayer Focus

1. Thank and praise God for all of the opportunities He has given you in life—those that you recognized and those that you didn't.

2. Ask God to forgive you for any and all opportunities you have wasted, ignored, or for which you did not give Him credit. Do not worry if you cannot remember or even recognize what they all were. God will forgive them all if you ask Him.

3. Ask God to help you be aware of the opportunities you have been given, but ignored. Do not fault God for the opportunities you missed. Never "blame" God.

4. Ask God to grant you peace about not being responsible for opportunities you are not given when you have done all you can to prepare for them.

5. Ask God to forgive you for looking down on other persons for not improving themselves when, in reality, those persons did not get certain opportunities (even if one of those persons was you).

6. Pray for the proper perspective concerning opportunities that come your way.

7. Praise Jesus for salvation that gives opportunities from God.

Steps to Take to Overcome Lie #22

1. Stop blaming God, yourself, or anyone else for opportunities you have not received. Blame does not solve anything. Recognizing the problems involved in the lack of all opportunities for everyone requires correction, when possible, understanding when not.

2. Start seeking opportunities that currently exist. Past opportunities are no longer opportunities. They are history.

3. Never stop searching for opportunities to improve yourself within God's will. Seek God's glory, not your own.

4. Of the current and future opportunities you discover, make a distinct list of the ones you would "like a shot at" that will be within God's will for your life. The others do not have application to your life. Do not envy any opportunities that are not God's will for your life.

5. Of the opportunities that would possibly fit in God's will for your life, make a list, prioritizing them from your most favorite to least favorite.

6. Find out what the qualifications are for those opportunities and how you can realistically attain those qualifications. Begin to make plans and commit to acquiring those qualifications.

7. On your list of steps to prepare for opportunities, try to accomplish as many steps that pre-

pare you for multiple choices. In other words, if two forms of preparation are equal in every way, but one would prepare you for two or more opportunities and the other wouldn't, choose the one that qualifies you for several opportunities.

8. Stop looking at opportunities emotionally; rather, look at them logically, maturely, and scripturally. Pray, learn, and practice accepting the reality of the numbers of opportunities versus the number of participants or hopefuls competing for those opportunities.

9. Compare any knowledge you have about opportunities, or lack of them, to what Jesus teaches about how to live and respond. If your views do not align with Scripture, they are wrong and harmful to your peace, hope, and future.

10. Strive to create opportunities for others whenever you can.

Lie #23: *"Winning Is All that Matters!"*

This definitely is not true in every situation. As a matter of fact, in situations of earthly competition the Bible does not declare that getting first place is all that matters! This is not to denigrate first place when it is achieved or achievable, but getting first place is not all that matters.

Would you like an example? How about several thousand examples? You don't have to look any farther than the Boston Marathon, or any marathon, for that matter. Yes, there are some professional or semi-professional athletes who approach such a race with the "First place is all that matters" attitude.

Watch any of these marathons, however, and you will eventually see why that philosophy only applies to a handful of people at the finish line. Actually, it only applies to a handful of people at the starting line! Out of the thousands of people at any marathon, usually less than a half-dozen runners have a chance at winning first place!

Then why are there thousands of other people in the race if they cannot win first place? Because getting first place is not all that matters! Thousands of people enjoy marathons, contests, and competitions with no intention, hope, or even desire to compete for first place. Why? Because first place is not all that matters!

Many people enter marathons and other competitions in life, happily knowing that they will not achieve first place. Many times they know that they will not get second, or third, or even one-hundredth place! Just participating in the event is worthwhile for many reasons.

Participating in an event or competition without winning can be fun! Participating without winning is exciting. Participating without winning helps to build experience! Participating without winning is educational. Participating without winning many times means making new friends. Participating, even without winning or placing, means enjoying life. Participation is its own reward.

Are you starting to get the picture that getting first place is not all that matters? You may be thinking, "Yes, but in those marathons, first place gets the most money!" That's true! As a matter of fact, most of the thousands of people in a marathon, not only don't win money but they have to pay entry fees. They pay their money knowing full well that they are not going to win money in return!

But money is not everything, just as winning first place is not everything. To win first place, runners must sacrifice hours, days, weeks, months, years, or even decades of other activities just to win, or even hope to win, only one marathon or specific competition in a lifetime!

Just like Olympic athletes, these competitors must sacrifice family time, social time, personal time and time for just about every other activity they might be interested in. Many people even sacrifice personal time with the Lord to achieve first place, to become a world champion, or to be an Olympic medallist.

Many times the thousands of people who participate in events, but never win or place, live much more happy, hopeful and balanced lives than those who idolize the first place prize.

Is it worth losing your husband or wife, your children, or friends, or a lifetime of other opportunities just to guarantee winning first place? It is not.

If you can win first place and maintain a biblically balanced perspective on life, that's great! There is nothing wrong with that; God does expect us to do our best in any given situation.

In many situations, however, the best we can do is to compete or participate with a biblical approach to balancing that competition with other important aspects of our lives!

Whether it's competing for the presidency of the United States, receiving a much-desired scholarship, winning first place at the science fair, or getting the highest-paying position in the office, getting first place is not all that matters! The *journey* to first place is just as important as getting the first place award.

Life goes on very well, even enjoyably, without first place. In almost every competition, the true winners in life are those who can compete and understand this at the same time!

If you are so driven that you must compete for a prize, find your true joy by seeking the same prize that the apostle Paul sought in Philippians 3:14. It is the one prize that counts for eternity!

Bible Verses to Overcome Lie #23

- "I press toward the mark for the prize of the high calling of God in Christ Jesus." Philippians 3:14 (KJV)

- "For what is a man profited, if he shall gain the whole world, and lose his own soul? or what shall a man give in exchange for his soul?" Matthew 16:26 (KJV)

Related Scripture Passages

- Matthew 16:24-38
- Matthew 19:16-30
- Luke 16:13
- Mark 9:34-37

Suggested Prayer Focus

1. Pray for the burden of seeking first place to be removed from you. This does not mean that you should never try for first place. It simply means that you should pray for the burden and strife of that effort to be removed.

2. Pray to gain a biblical perspective concerning competition for glory's sake.

3. Pray to gain a biblical perspective concerning competition for survival's sake or the sake of accomplishing goals within God's will.

4. Pray for discernment about when you should compete for a top-ranked position, and when to compete for participation, not position.

5. Pray for peace and healthy, biblically grounded acceptance concerning not "placing" in any certain event or competition.

6. Pray that you will desire priorities in life that are aligned with Scripture.

7. Praise God for being allowed to compete in any competition you ever 'lost.' (Praise Him for your victories, too!)

8. Praise God for the joy that the winner or winners who "defeat" you will experience.

9. Pray that all of your actions in any competition you enter will honor Jesus.

10. Pray for God's will in your life before deciding to enter any competition.

11. Pray for God's will to be done before the competition starts. In your heart, dedicate your efforts and the competition's outcome to the glory of Jesus and God.

12. Pray during competitions where there is time for your mind to pray while competing. Do not

pray to win. Rather, pray for God to receive glory through your efforts and participation.

13. Pray for the safety of all persons involved in the competition.

14. Pray for the spiritual, physical, and mental well-being of all those involved to be intact when the competition is over. Include yourself in this prayer.

15. Pray for God to receive all honor and glory for the results.

Steps to Take to Overcome Lie #23

1. Strive simply to compete at your best possible level. The rest is out of your hands. You should find your peace in knowing that you gave your best, not in believing that you are "outdoing" others.

2. Start to seek your joy in participation, instead of just winning. If you end up in first place, that's just "icing on the cake."

3. Do not enter competitions where "losing" will make you lose your hope, make you angry, rude, pout, or any other action that will not honor Jesus. Pray that you will no longer have these feelings in any challenge.

4. Do not enter competitions that will destroy your witness as a Christian.

5. Do not enter competitions based on non-Christian ideals or sinful activities.

6. In any competition, seek friendship and opportunities to witness for Christ to those friends.

7. Strive to find scriptural balance in your life.

8. Praise God, Jesus, and the Holy Spirit for the results of any competition you enter, even those you lose.

Lie #24:
"Doctors Are Better than Fry Cooks!"

Who in the world ever said such a lie, and how in the world would it affect anyone other than doctors and fry cooks? Like many of the other hope-destroying lies, this might have never been said out loud by anyone, but it is implied and acted upon by almost everyone.

Do you personally remember ever hearing someone say, "Doctors are better than fry cooks?" Probably not. On the other hand, have you ever seen storybooks, television shows, movies, plays, print advertising or commercials where it is portrayed or implied that doctors, lawyers, police officers, members of congress, presidents, movie stars, or sports stars are better than fry cooks, gas station attendants, store clerks, dishwashers, or any number of "blue collar" workers? Of course you have!

In the movies, the other media, and in everyday life, we are bombarded with the idea that "white collar" work and "professional" jobs are better or more glorious than others; therefore, people who have those jobs are better than others.

Just look at the way the word "professional" is often associated with doctors, lawyers, accountants, business executives, entrepreneurs, and other white collar jobs. The term is not often associated with store clerks, warehouse personnel, fry cooks, waiters or waitresses, valets, or many other service workers.

Do those who are not associated with the term "professional" work merely for the sake of having a hobby? Of course not! Are they also expected to do an expert job at what they do? Yes! Do they not deserve respect for doing their jobs in a "professional" and honest manner? Yes, they do deserve respect. They too are professionals!

But before we get too judgmental on how the media represents this problem, how do we ourselves view the lie, "Doctors are better than fry cooks?" When you were young, were you or are you even now more impressed with those youth who said, "I want to be a doctor when I grow up"? Would you get that same warm feeling if your six-year-old or your teenager announced at church, "I want to cook hamburgers for a living when I grow up"?

Would you brag any more on your children, parents, sons-in-law, or daughters-in-law, if they were doctors, lawyers, politicians, fashion models, or pilots than you would if they were garbage workers, street cleaners, or the people that pick up leftover fat at meat markets to deliver it for use in manufacturing? In all honesty, you would probably brag much more about the first group of workers!

That is why it is such a major hope-destroying lie, even if it is rarely spoken aloud. All of us, at times, believe it or respond to it by treating others with the notion that "Doctors are better than fry cooks," in mind. Others may also determine how they will treat us based on that same false belief.

If a man or woman has a job that God has allowed them to have, and we mock them, ignore them, mistreat them, or look down on them, we are doing the same to God; for He is the One who provided that job.

Jesus says in Scripture, about our treatment of others:

> Verily I say unto you, Inasmuch as ye have done it unto one of the least of these my brethren, ye have done it unto me (Matthew 25:40, KJV).

When you look down on someone because of that person's job, or because of the person's lack of employment, or you esteem one person higher than the other simply because of the type of work they do, you rob the hope of many people.

You rob the hope of those who presently do not have the "glamour" jobs by telling them with your actions, "You will not be worthy until you attain a certain job." At the same time, by treating any person or group of people that way, you teach the next generation to carry on the same lie.

Jesus Christ, the King of Kings and Lord of Lords worked as a carpenter while He was on earth. Would you have looked down on Him if you perceived Him according to your present standards?

The Son of God was a carpenter and honored God while doing. Therefore, you can do anything within God's will and greatly serve and honor God!

Bible Verses to Overcome Lie #24

- "Whatsoever thy hand findeth to do, do it with thy might..." Ecclesiastes 9:10 (KJV)

- "And whatsoever ye do, do it heartily, as to the Lord, and not unto men; Knowing that of the Lord ye shall receive the reward of the inheritance: for ye serve the Lord Christ." Colossians 3:23-24 (KJV)

Related Scripture Passages

- Matthew 9:9-13
- Mark 1
- Mark 6:1-4
- Luke 1, 2

Suggested Prayer Focus

1. Ask for forgiveness for any time you have had less than Christ-like thoughts or have treated someone in a less than Christ-like manner because of his or her job.

2. Praise God for all forms of work and for all the people who are willing to work at whatever assignment God has given them as a vocation.

3. Pray to see each person and his or her job or station in life through the compassionate eyes of Jesus, not according to shallow human standards.

4. Praise God for those people who are willing to take on the tough, dirty or unrewarding jobs of this world. Pray for God to abundantly bless them and reward them.

5. Pray for the Holy Spirit to move people to behave kindly toward those who are mistreated.

6. Pray that you will treat everyone in a Christ-like manner regardless of his or her occupation or status of employment.

7. Pray to speak only compassionate words in conversations about work, workers, and what they must endure.

8. Pray that you will not continue thinking that one profession or line of work makes one person more valuable than another.

Steps to Take to Overcome Lie #24

1. Always treat workers of any kind, as well as the unemployed, in the way you would want to be treated in their position.

2. Avoid statements about occupations that include the phrase, "just a...." For example, "He (she) is only a fry cook."

3. Do not look down on yourself or anyone else because of your present line of work.

4. Do not apologize for any type of honest work that you do.

5. Do not teach children or young people to look down on any type of biblically acceptable job, or to glorify others because they have jobs that yield a certain amount of status.

6. Do not teach children or your people to look down on the people who have less than biblically acceptable jobs. Teach them to pray for those people.

7. Do not make jokes that denigrate people because of their occupation.

8. Sign up for and perform volunteer work that will get you dirty, exhausted, or possibly even be made fun of, but that will help someone. This will help you to be more compassionate toward them in the future.

9. Be considerate of those who provide a service to you. For instance, stack trash neatly in proper containers for the garbage collectors. Put unwanted items in the trash can in your hotel room and neatly collect and place dirty towels where they belong. Leave your dirty plates and dishes in a neat manner for the bus persons who work in restaurants. Wipe your crumbs onto a plate. Clean up after activities at church and be considerate of the custodian.

10. Begin to evaluate how movie or television characters are wrongly or rudely treated or portrayed on screen. Make a commitment not to treat anyone in that way.

11. Read about men and women in the Bible who had "blue collar" jobs and realize that you would be treating them rudely also. Remember, Jesus was a carpenter.

12. Be aware that you might be guilty of treating people badly or rudely simply because they have a good job or one that is "better" than your own. Remember, white collar workers are often abused, looked down on, or even hated, specifically because of the kind of work that they do.

Lie #25:
"Horoscopes and psychics are harmless!"

Don't count on it! Don't count on any of it. Don't even mess around with it. Don't do it for fun, and don't experiment with it. The entire industry is based on lies, false prophets, and evil spirits.

Do you think that this is an exaggeration? The Bible clearly speaks against sorcerers, magicians, diviners, enchanters, false prophets, astrologers, monthly prognosticators, star gazers, sooth sayers, witchcraft, spirits, wizards, divination, and necromancers (those who seek to communicate with the dead).

Nowhere in the Bible does it record that these things are entertaining, acceptable, or innocent. In fact, the Bible makes it very clear that these are ungodly, evil, sinful activities that will bring the wrath of God on all who participate. God's Word says that you will be defiled by these things.

Do you want to be looked upon as defiled in the eyes of God, or unclean, worthy of the wrath of God, or in danger of the fire of hell? The Bible uses all of these words to describe those who seek such sources of instruction, guidance, or communication.

Doing such things as reading your horoscope, calling a psychic, or having your palm or Tarot cards read by a fortune teller fall within the list of things that God strictly forbids and for which He promises His wrath.

Saying or believing, "I just do it for fun," about something God says is so utterly evil and wrong is about the same as saying, "I just worship Satan for fun." All of those things listed are of Satan, and it mocks God for you to seek their guidance, instruction, or help in any fashion.

The Bible commands in Deuteronomy 18:9-12:

> When thou art come into the land which the Lord thy God giveth thee, thou shalt not learn to do after the abominations of those nations. There shall not be found among you any one that maketh his son or his daughter to pass through the fire, or that useth divination, or an observer of times, or an enchanter, or a witch, Or a charmer, or a consulter with familiar spirits, or a wizard, or a necromancer. For all that do these things are an abomination unto the Lord (KJV)

Did you see the first part of that passage of Scripture? We are not even to "...learn to do..." those "abominations...." That is a pretty stern and clear commandment from God!

If you play with, experiment with, or participate in those things, even "just for fun," you have already learned those ways. Every day that you continue to indulge in those activities, from that day forward, you will be choosing purposefully to deny God's command.

Horoscopes and all such activity literally steal the hope of those who depend on them for guidance and answers to life's dilemmas. They take our hope in God and place it in the hands of God's enemy, Satan, and Satan's followers. They take our hope from Jesus, who is the Truth, and put our hope for the day, the week, the month, the future in the hands of the "father of lies," Satan.

When the horoscope warns you of a bad day, it steals your hope, based strictly on a lie from those who are directly disobeying God. When they promise you good things, it is an outright lie from someone the Bible shows clearly is a false prophet. Hope based on lies is false hope and eventually blinds us to true hope in Jesus.

If you are relying on astrologers or their horoscopes, psychics, card readers, palm readers or spiritualists to show you the future, your association with them in any way would bring the wrath of God on you. Continued reliance on them, while knowing that God strictly forbids it and says it is of Satan, might call into question your very salvation. That does not sound like hope in any fashion!

Any and all details you need to know about the future, God has already given to you in the Bible, not in the newspaper, nor in cards or a crystal ball.

God forbids us to seek contact with the dead. True hope is among the living, and godly, true life is in Jesus! The stars can't even control their own destiny, much less anyone else's. The future is not in a crystal ball nor your palms. The future is in God's hands only!

Bible Verses to Overcome Lie #25

* "Regard not them that have familiar spirits, neither seek after wizards, to be defiled by them: I am the LORD your God." Leviticus 19:31 (KJV)

* "And the soul that turneth after such as have familiar spirits, and after wizards, to go a whoring after them, I will even set my face against that soul, and will cut him off from among his people." Leviticus 20:6 (KJV)

Related Scripture Passages

* 1 Thessalonians 5:22
* Romans 12:9
* Matthew 13-16
* Psalm 37

Suggested Prayer Focus

1. Pray for God to reveal to you any evil that you may unknowingly be participating in, thinking that it is innocent.

2. Pray for the Holy Spirit to overpower any evil that you have been associating with, knowingly or unknowingly.

3. Ask God to forgive you for your sins associated with that evil activity.

4. If you have never given your life to Jesus, confess with your mouth to Jesus right now that you are a sinner. Repent of your sin. Believe that He died and was raised. Give Jesus complete control of your life as your Savior and Lord. Believe the words of the apostle Paul, "'The word is near you; it is in your mouth and in your heart,' that is, the word of faith we are proclaiming: That if you confess with your mouth, 'Jesus is Lord,' and believe in your heart that God raised him from the dead, you will be saved" (Romans 10:8-9).

5. If you are sure you are already saved, and you ask for forgiveness for these sins, accept God's forgiveness through Jesus and do those things no more!

Steps to Take to Overcome Lie #25

1. Do not read horoscopes, either for real advice or for fun. God forbids it and promises His wrath upon all who do such.

2. Do not call psychics, or visit them, or contact them on the Internet, or by mail, or through any other means. If they were real psychics, and knew you needed help, they would be calling you!

3. Do not use spiritualists in any way for any reason. As a Christian, the only Spirit you should have in your life is the Holy Spirit of God.

4. Do not attempt to contact the dead or be present when someone else is attempting to do so.

5. Do not participate in, watch, or have any involvement in seances, speaking to ghosts, or activity that calls on spirits or demons.

6. Do not get involved with anything satanic.

7. If you have them, remove from your surroundings and your life pentagrams or any object associated with satanism, devil worship, or demon worship.

8. Remove from your surrounding and life anything used by spiritualists, soothsayers, and demonologists.

9. Remove from your surroundings anything associated with witchcraft, witches, or warlocks.

10. Physically remove crystal balls from your property and your life.

11. Physically remove from your property and your life Tarot cards or any other items used for telling the future.

12. Physically remove from your property and your life Ouija® Boards, demon games, and role-playing games that involve wizardry or witchcraft of any kind.

13. Physically remove all astrology and horoscope paraphernalia from your property and your life. Do not read your horoscope in your newspapers or in magazines.

14. Seek the counsel of a pastor or Christian counselor if you have trouble releasing these things from your life.

15. Commit to serious, urgent, and unrelenting prayer and Bible study about such things if you are leery of counsel against them, or if you still believe that they are harmless and just for "fun."

Lie #26:
"I Can't Afford the Help I Need!"

This is one of those "close-enough-to-the-truth-but-not-really-the-truth" lies! Let's face it, certain kinds of help do indeed cost money, but not all help!

If Satan can convince you that all help costs money, and you have little or no money, he can defeat you before you make one move! As a matter of fact, you are very likely not to even attempt to seek help if you have no money and believe you need it.

This is a great way for Satan to oppress everyone, from the extremely poor and homeless, to the middle class, to those hanging by a thread to the end of their budget, and to those hovering just above financial failure or bankruptcy.

If you have little or no money beyond what you need for essentials, it can be very depressing and hope-destroying to believe you can't even afford to ask for help. It is a belief that you will need God's help to overcome. In all reality, turning to God is the greatest help you can have that does not cost you money! In fact, even if you had all the money in the world, you could not afford to buy His help. God's help is worth more than money. His help is priceless, as is His love for you!

Seeking God's help and guidance is the most prudent, wise, and profitable thing you can do to help yourself through any situation. If you have no money, or have limited resources to seek help, this is the time, the day, and the very moment for you to stop, pray, and seek God-given help in your life!

Whether your present situation is by your own making or by circumstances beyond your control, you may need God now more than at any other time in your life. No one wants to help you more, and no one on earth can help you more than God!

Does that mean God will just drop help in your lap and everything will be fine? It's possible, but that is not very likely! So what should you pray for to begin to get the help you need?

First of all, if you have not already given control of your life to Jesus Christ, you must do that! Only a born-again believer has the promise that God will hear his or her prayers. You must confess that you are a sinner, repent of your sins (that means having a true desire to turn from a sinful life and turn from that life), and ask Jesus to take control of your life and be your Lord! If you ask Jesus to be the Lord of your life, He will!

If you have already done that, you need to pray that God will grant you wisdom, guidance, strength, protection, and grace, as well as your physical needs. If you have access to a Bible, you need to ask God to let the Holy Spirit guide you to verses that you need to read this very day. If you can't afford a Bible, ask a church for one.

In Scripture reading and prayer, ask God for wisdom to find and recognize where some of the helpful places are. Pray for urgent help. Ask the Lord to give you wisdom to recognize who will help you versus who will try to take advantage of you. Ask God to guide you to a church to join.

Ask God to guide your every step to the very doors you must go through, and the exact words to say as you seek help! Pray that you will feel Jesus' presence with you as you need Him most. Ask God to have the Holy Spirit guide your eyes and hands as you flip through the telephone book to find help. Pray for your eyes to see and your ears to hear the messages, broadcasts, or commercials that will lead you to places and persons that can help you. Ask God to guide your hands as you search for Christian radio or television stations and programs, or even Christian materials that someone has donated for those in need.

Pray for God to begin to touch the hearts of anyone and everyone He would have to help you. Pray for the Holy Spirit to give you the courage, strength, and trust to talk to the right people. Pray for a divine "hedge of protection" around you and your family or friends while you seek help. Pray for the strength to do the right thing.

Ask God to bind Satan and any demonic activity that would hinder you from seeking and receiving help. Ask for God's grace, which means admitting that you really do need God's help, even if you believe you don't deserve it, or even if you only feel you don't deserve it right now.

You can begin your search for help by contacting local Christian churches or ministry organizations, the YMCA, the Salvation Army, a local Christian mission, or any other Christian group you can find. Search the Yellow Pages® and contact places you learn about on the radio and television.

Before you start searching, pray sincerely for direction. Once you have prayed and are truly ready to begin the task ahead, by God's power start your search for help.

If you trust God, help will certainly come! God can send aid in a number of mysterious ways. There is much help available that does not cost you money. Prayer is the best help to get you started!

Bible Verses to Overcome Lie #26

- "But I am poor and needy; yet the Lord thinketh upon me: thou art my help and my deliverer; make no tarrying, O my God." Psalm 40:17 (KJV)

- "For thou art my rock and my fortress; therefore for thy name's sake lead me, and guide me." Psalm 31:3 (KJV)

Related Scripture Passages

- Psalm 46
- Psalm 33
- Psalm 54
- Psalm 35

Suggested Prayer Focus

1. Pray for the courage and the humility to accept help that you cannot afford.

2. Pray for the Lord to lead you to a church, agency, or person who will give you a Bible if you do not have one. Remember, if you have the money to spend on any type of entertainment, you have money to purchase a Bible. If not, God would expect you to accept a free one.

3. Pray for urgent help for your situation.

4. Pray for wisdom to distinguish true help from cons or scams.

5. Pray for the Holy Spirit to guide your steps to the right places for help.

6. Pray for the right words to say when asking for help for your problem.

7. Pray that you will receive mercy and compassion from the people you ask for help. Pray that all of their suggestions, requests, or requirements will be only those that are within God's will.

8. Pray for a humble spirit to accept help, yet to have God-given courage at the same time.

9. Pray for the integrity to use free resources in a Christ-like way and as a good steward.

Steps to Take to Overcome Lie #26

1. Start with the most helpful sources—prayer and the Bible. If you can't afford anything else, you can always afford to pray.

2. Use any free time you have to read the entire Book of Proverbs before you take any other steps for help. No other advice in the world, for a fee or for free, will give you more wisdom than the advice given in Proverbs.

3. Continue to read portions of Proverbs daily (and any other passages the Holy Spirit directs you to read) as you continue your search for help and after you receive your help.

4. Contact your pastor or a local church for advice about local organizations that offer the type of help you need.

5. Ask the pastor or other resource person where you can receive help for your most immediate need. If the church can provide it, they will offer. If they can't, they likely will know of a place and will direct you to it.

6. Many churches can provide emergency assistance in the form of food, shelter, utility payments, shelter from spousal abuse, or some type of emergency financial need. Most churches will not give cash for any reason, but they will guide you as much as they can, or guide you to the proper place to receive help.

7. Refrain from asking anyone from the church or organization to give you money. Instead, let them know what you need the money for and they will set about helping you. The money is not really what you need, but the item. If they know what the item is, they can direct you to the right resources to get that item.

8. If you still believe you need money for something, ask the pastor or other ministry resource person for the names of any organizations that can provide financial assistance if you desperately need it.

9. Commit to looking in the telephone book and in magazines or brochures for any additional help you need.

10. Look under the heading of "missions," or under "Christian Organizations." You may also look under the heading of "relief agencies."

11. If you do not find assistance under general headings, look for the Red Cross, United Way, Salvation Army, and YMCA or YWCA.

12. Look for financial counseling and free training programs.

Lie #27: *"Image Is Everything!"*

This is the lie of a self-absorbed generation. In the land of glitter, glamour, "photo ops," public relations management, image consulting, websites, sound bites, fashion trends, best and worst dressed lists, team logos, what's-in-and-what's-out, and keeping up with the Joneses, it's very easy to get caught up in trying to impress just about anyone and everyone.

It is very easy for us to fall into the trap of trying to impress everyone. From the very early developmental stages, we begin to recognize that people treat us better when they are impressed or pleased with us. Mommy and Daddy hug us more, laugh more, and hold us more when we are impressing them with cuteness than when they are unimpressed.

The need to impress others is further confirmed when we go to kindergarten, grade school, and even Sunday school, and we begin to realize that the cutest or best dressed students get all the attention. In junior high, high school, and college, those with the best "wise cracks," funniest insults, latest fashions, highest grades, or highest sports averages are the ones who get the attention.

Day by day, year by year, it is ingrained into our psyches and our egos that in order to be liked, loved, welcomed, cheered, popular or successful, we must impress anyone and everyone in one way or another.

When we are "successful" in our efforts to attain status and impress others, things seem to go right for us. But when we fail in our efforts to impress, or when we impress in ways that lead to trouble, pain, or punishment, we begin to see the consequences of those actions and lose hope.

It is not always possible to be the cutest—and if our looks don't happen to fit the latest trend that defines "good-looking," any hopes we had for getting attention for our looks are dashed. If being funny is what "works," and we're not particularly funny or witty, we can say "Good-bye, hope." If we cannot afford the latest fashions or our bodies don't fit into trendy sizes, we must say "Good-bye" to any hope we had of being noticed for our clothes. If we cannot make the highest grades, excel in sports, land the most prestigious job, drive the best car, or make the most money, we are forced to bid "Good-bye, hope" to our desire to gain attention for those things!

The real good-bye to hope, however, does not come when we fail to impress any particular person; rather, it comes the moment we switch our hope from Jesus to anything else. Real hope only comes from God.

If we pin our hope on impressing others, we have already exchanged real God-given hope for temporary false hope.

Even if you can impress some of the people some of the time, you can't impress all of the people all of the time; and sometimes you can't impress any of the people any of the time. When you fail to impress someone, and your hope is based on being impressive, you have set yourself up for a great fall. When that fall happens, you are even less impressive, then more destroyed, and again, "Good-bye, hope."

Satan is aware that we cannot impress everyone all of the time. He uses it against each of us to deceive us into taking our eyes off of the only One who judges us with mercy, grace, and love—Jesus Christ.

God does not expect us to impress Him. We cannot outdo Jesus and His perfection. We are expected only to serve the Lord in the best way we can each day, one day at a time, in the situations that God allows for our lives.

God already knows that we will fail Him at times, but He will forgive us every time we ask Him. He loves us and will always love us, in spite of our failures and shortcomings.

If we live for Christ, we know that many people will be offended. That means they won't be impressed with us. If we do good and give God all the glory, they will be impressed with God and still won't be impressed with us. If we do wrong, we will suffer God's wrath, discipline, and judgment, and they still won't be impressed!

God has blessed us with the Bible by instructing us to live in ways for which we will be rewarded greatly in heaven by God. But we are also promised that the world will not be impressed, and they will literally persecute us for what they think of us and who we represent, Jesus.

Living in ways that please God and not to impress the world is something for which we have permission from God. Jesus promises in the Book of Matthew that pleasing God is a way of life that is a blessing and a reason to be glad!

Bible Verses to Overcome Lie #27

- "Blessed are ye, when men shall revile you, and persecute you, and shall say all manner of evil against you falsely, for my sake. Rejoice, and be exceeding glad: for great is your reward in heaven: for so persecuted they the prophets which were before you." Matthew 5:11,12 (KJV)

- "...for the LORD seeth not as man seeth; for man looketh on the outward appearance, but the LORD looketh on the heart." 1 Samuel 16:7 (KJV)

Related Scripture Passages

- John 15:18-21
- John 17
- 1 Corinthians 1
- James 1

Suggested Prayer Focus

1. Pray to stop competing with "the Joneses," worrying about trends, or trying to impress everyone, or even anyone.

2. Pray to understand the need to do things because it is God's desire and according to Jesus' teachings, not because you are trying to impress anyone, even your brothers and sisters in Christ.

3. Pray to understand that, as believers, we are to lead others to Christ and impact their lives by reflecting His love and His greatness, not by trying to impress them with our own.

4. Pray to understand that when things are done within God's will, it isn't important who was impressed or offended by it. Pray to do the right thing simply because it is God's will.

5. Pray for strength, courage, and stamina to live a Christlike life, knowing you are not to glory in or worry trying to impress others.

Steps to Take to Overcome Lie #27

1. Commit to understand that living the way Jesus teaches might impress some people, but that is not your goal or concern. You must understand that doing the right thing because it is right has nothing to do with whether or not people are impressed. Until you distinguish between the

two, you will be a slave to actions designed to impress others.

2. Commit to make choices in every situation based on your understanding of what the Bible teaches is right, not on what you believe will impress someone.

3. Commit to make choices among your friends based on what is right according to the Bible, not what is impressive. Also commit to make choices for or within your family based on what the Bible mandates is right, not according to what is impressive.

4. Commit to make choices at work or school based on what is right, not based on what will impress the boss, teacher, or friends.

5. Commit to make choices at church based on what the Bible says is right, not on what you think will impress the preacher, deacons, or anyone else you might want to impress at church.

6. Strive to understand that sometimes when you attempt to live right by following the wisdom of the Bible, other people might be offended and persecute you. When they do, it is with God's permission that they do so. He will give you grace to overcome.

7. Likewise, strive to understand that when you do what is right because God wants you to, He

may allow people to be impressed. That is not a sin. It is a gift from God to allow you to be rewarded sometimes, in His measure and at His will. It becomes a sin when you strive for, or make decisions based on that moment of glory or measure of impression to be directed at you.

8. Do not buy things to impress others in any way. Buy things because you need them or enjoy them, not because you think someone will be impressed by them. Do not buy things to win love or friendship. That is a very costly and neverending approach to finding love or friendship that isn't real in the first place.

Lie #28:
"I'll Never Be Loved!"

No pun intended, but this is probably the most "hateful" lie that Satan can use against anyone. Not only will you one day receive the love you desire, you should know that you are already loved right now, and not just by anyone! You are loved unconditionally right now by God! You are loved beyond measure by Jesus Christ!

God loved you while you were still a sinner. The Bible reveals in Romans 5:8:

> But God commendeth his love toward us, in that, while we were yet sinners, Christ died for us.

That means even if you have never given your life to Jesus, God loves you already, even in your sin!

The Bible teaches that God does not approve of your sin, but He loves you right now! He loves you so much that He allowed His only Son, Jesus, to die for your sin and the sins of all the people of the world! Jesus loves you so much, He was willing to be punished for your sins and all the sins of the world, and to die on the cross to save the world. Because He is God's Son, He came back to life from the grave after three days, ascend to heaven, and lives forever!

If you don't know His love, you must be born again. All you must do to be born again is:

(1) confess that you are a sinner;

(2) repent of your sins;

(3) give Jesus control of your life by accepting Him as Lord. It is a free gift of salvation. It is a free gift of love, the greatest love ever!

Right now you may be wondering, "What if I already know all of that and Satan has robbed me of the joy and hope that God's love should bring me? What do you need to do then?

First, you need to stop, pray, and recognize in your heart what that love means for your life and for your eternity. After, and only after, you truly recognize what that love means in your life should you approach God about any human love you might be seeking.

What if you are telling yourself, "I know God loves me, but no one else does or ever will"? That is a lie from the father of lies, Satan. He has planted that thought in your heart and mind. If you are willing to trust God, you will see that it is a lie.

God is love. God dwells in the hearts of every true Christian, and true Christians love those whom God loves. That means you!

Someone loves you! Many people love you as a brother or sister in Christ. That is better than any "love" outside of Christ.

What if even that kind of love is not what you are talking about? What if you are still asking God, "Who will really love me for his/her own?" Only God can answer that question; but there are questions you can answer that will help you to see the truth about the kind of love you are seeking.

Answer some of the following questions now, and use your answers to determine whether you can see hope for that kind of love in the future:

- If you showed the kind of love that forgives others, even when they treat you wrong, would it be likely that someone would love you in return?

- If you showed the kind of love that is patient, would it be likely that someone would love you in return?

- If you showed the kind of love that is understanding, would it be likely that someone would love you in return?

- If you showed the kind of love that does not envy, would it be likely that someone would love you in return?

- If you showed the kind of love that does not easily anger, would it be likely that someone would love you in return?

- If you showed the kind of love that God has shown you, would it be likely that someone would love you in return?

If you are honest, the answer to all those questions is "Yes!" If you truly love as the Bible teaches that Jesus loves us, then according to your own honest answers, it is very likely that someone will love you in return!

If you surround those around you in God's love, you will be surrounded by people surrounded by God's love. Think about that!

Bible Verses to Overcome Lie #28

- "And we have known and believed the love that God hath to us. God is love; and he that dwelleth in love dwelleth in God, and God in him." 1 John 4:16 KJV)

- "Mercy unto you, and peace and love, be multiplied." Jude 1:2 (KJV)

Related Scripture Passages

- 1 John

Suggested Prayer Focus

1. Pray to feel and accept the love that God and His Son Jesus have already given, continues to give, and will always give to you.

2. Pray to be able to express that love to others through testimony, witness, and actions.

3. Pray to find more hope in the love you will give than in love you are hoping to receive.

4. Pray for God to reveal those around you who need the love of Christ in their lives.

5. Pray for ways to minister to those people according to their needs as Jesus would have you to minister.

6. Pray to understand the difference between Christ-like love and love that expects something in return.

7. Concerning love between you and someone you might marry, pray for true God-ordained love, not lust, to prevail.

8. Begin praying for God to prepare the heart and guide the path of any person with whom He would have you "fall in love."

9. Pray for peace and strength in knowing only the love of Christ during times when you cannot find or recognize love from others.

Steps to Take to Overcome Lie #28

1. If feeling loved is a high priority right now, commit to change that priority to sharing Christ's love with others.

2. You will have to commit to repeated, frequent, and ongoing attempts to think about things other than "finding" love.

3. Try to find seminars about Christian love, relationships, and self-esteem from a Christian perspective. Enroll in and attend as many of them as you are able.

4. Begin to be aware of your own actions toward everyone around you.

5. Throughout the day, if possible (or at night when not), make a list of the different ways you have treated people or reacted to them in their presence. Make a note of any actions that would make you feel less than loving toward anyone who has treated you that way.

6. Commit to reducing those actions on a daily and ongoing basis.

7. Throughout the day, or before going to sleep each night, make a list of opportunities to show Christ's love, or "be His hands" to someone whom you missed or ignored. Commit to look for those opportunities each day. Do something to show His love or "be His hands" by serving or helping those who need it.

8. Make a list of your own habits that might be annoying to others. Commit to find ways to stop those habits. The purpose of this is not to impress others, but to be considerate and show respect for the privilege of bearing the name "Christian" in your life.

9. Commit to recognizing the difference between love and lust. Work within God's will to be a person to be loved. Don't work to "win" love with lustful measures.

10. Write down your expectations concerning what you hope to receive from someone who would love you. Determine if those expectations line up with Scripture or are only selfish wants.

11. Write down what you plan to bring into a relationship. What can you offer to someone you love? Ask God to remove any selfish wants from your heart and mind.

Lie #29: *"I'll Do It on My Own!"*

Could this be called the lie of the "pride of independence?" This may well be a lie that is most specifically maintained within American culture more than any other. In other words, the saying, "A man's home is his castle," has left us all, men and women alike, hungering for a little kingdom of our own. The selfish slang term, "my space" has practically made the concept of sharing housing seem like a disease.

It is mostly an American idea that when you become a legal adult, you move out, move on, and move up. Reversing any of those stages, even temporarily, is perceived as failure and cause for shame.

To their benefit, this concept is not as prevalent in many other cultures. Actually, the concept of family members sharing property, land, houses, or even tents, has scriptural approval in many of the Bible stories of God's people. In many cases, the shared lives of several generations of one family is not uncommon.

Today, shared family housing is still acceptable, practical, and even most honorable, in Asia, the Middle East, Africa, Europe, and some South American countries. Because of the blending of cultures, even in the United States, some cultures that have traditionally shared family housing, still do so honorably.

How does Satan trick anyone who would feel shame when needing to move in with someone for help? He uses pride, arrogance, unbiblical levels of self-esteem, and selfishness to distort our views of life, success, and worth.

It is actually wise for generations of a family to pool income, share expenses, protect, and care for each other, when possible. Pooling resources leaves more money for education, food, medical expenses, and even entertainment when life's responsibilities are shared.

Helping each other by sharing resources can give senior family members the joy of sharing wisdom with the young, and it can give the young an opportunity to gain much knowledge, without having to learn it from their own mistakes.

Many times families who cannot afford to send their sons and daughters away to college and expensive dorms can afford for them to attend college locally by having the children live at home. Many doctors, lawyers, mechanics, welders, and others have completed their education and training programs while staying or returning home to live.

There is scriptural basis for, and accounts of, people staying with others or being helped by others for varying lengths of time—from a single night to months or years at a time. Even Mary and Joseph accepted lodging in a stable, which held the manger where Jesus was born.

The disciples often stayed in the homes of other Christians. Moving families and tribes traveled and stayed together to get to where God would have them or to where troubles drove them.

Were Mary and Joseph losers? No! Were the disciples losers? No! Were God's people losers? No! Was Jesus a loser? God forbid!

When you refuse the help of friends or family, or even of institutions, you may be refusing the help of God! The Bible teaches that to avoid work is wrong; but to deny help or a place to stay when needed can only be explained by the sin of pride!

Who is trying to help you right now by offering you a place to stay or some other form of assistance? Are you turning them down for reasons other than safety or other practical concern? Are you guilty of pride or arrogance? Is it all right for God's people to stay with others in times of need, but you think that you are too good for that? If so, then you need to ask for forgiveness and accept their help graciously as it comes from God! Then, do your part to make things better!

Are you ashamed to accept help? Don't be! God does not ask, or even want, shame from you! He loves you and He is offering His help through those who can provide it.

If someone known to be trustworthy offers to help you—a place to stay, work, food, or any other need that you have—do not be too proud or ashamed to accept that help if, after praying, you are confident that the offer is safe. It is a gift from God!

God is not likely to drop manna from heaven for you, but He promises to provide your every need. Sometimes God will meet our needs by sending others to come to our aid. When God sends help, often it is not in the form we expect. The form of help God chooses to send may have a hidden, additional benefit to you or someone else.

Bible Verses to Overcome Lie #29

- "John answered and said, A man can receive nothing, except it be given him from heaven." John 3:27 (KJV)

- "Though the LORD be high, yet hath he respect unto the lowly: but the proud he knoweth afar off." Psalm 138:6 (KJV)

Related Scripture Passages

- Matthew 10
- Acts 11:32
- Proverbs 21
- James 4:6

Suggested Prayer Focus

1. Pray for the removal of the sin of pride or arrogance when it prevails.

2. Praise and thank God for any help offered, remembering that God sends help out of love.

3. Pray for discernment to know when a situation is safe enough to accept the help that comes through it.

4. Pray for blessings upon the house or place where you receive your help. Pray for blessings on those who have made it possible.

5. Pray for a hedge of protection around the place and the people while you are among them. Pray also for those who will help you even after you leave their physical presence.

6. Pray for those who have no home or food, or some other need, and no one to help them get the things they need.

7. Pray to recognize the benefits to all when families or friends in need share their resources.

8. Pray for God to provide the resources you need for independent living if and when it is in His will.

9. Ask Jesus to comfort you when you must accept the help of others. Pray for those who have no one to help them.

10. Pray for the courage to help others and share with them when they need it. Pray for God's protection around you and your family during that time. Pray for God to be honored in all ways during that time.

Steps to Take to Overcome Lie #29

1. Mathematics makes this one obvious. If you don't have enough money to live in your own place, it is better for you to stay with someone else. If someone else is broke, they need help, too.

2. If you are considering moving in with either your parents or children for a long-term stay, calculations will help you decide. If all or anyone in the discussion comes out ahead by one of you staying with the others, and all parties agree, pray about the decision and move forward if you feel it's God's will.

3. Use logic and biblical instruction to evaluate your situation and determine the extent of help you need from others or them from you.

4. Study other cultures who share housing and other resources between family members and friends in need. Note any positive results as a matter of perspective; negative results for ways to avoid them.

5. Do not mock others or make light of their situation when it is "their turn" to go to someone else for help. It will make them lose hope and dignity in their time of need. And if your turn comes around, your words, thoughts, and actions will haunt you or someone you know.

6. If you are a parent, do not constantly talk about or dream of the day when "the kids move out."

It will cause them to feel guilty or shameful if they cannot move out on "schedule" or if they must return.

7. Those same words could haunt your parents as they become seniors and need your help. Consider that you, too, will one day become senior (or disabled) and need the help of your children, grandchildren, family, or friends.

8. Approach each situation as if Jesus is directly affected by your decision to offer or receive help.

9. Make anyone who needs your extended or long-term assistance feel safe, secure, and welcome as if they are going forward with the compassion and love of Jesus Christ Himself. As His ambassadors, this is how it should be.

Lie #30: *"I Can't Make a Difference in the World!"*

Your life has already made a difference in the world! From the day you were conceived, until long after you draw your last earthly breath, you will have had an affect on the lives of scores of people.

If you feel that you have not lived such a "great life," it may be because you have not always made a *positive* difference in this world, but you have made a difference already. What you need to do today is recognize that everything you do makes a difference. Then, live positively and with that knowledge in mind for the rest of your life.

From the second you were conceived, you began to make chemical, hormonal, and biological differences in your mother's life. As the months passed, her life with you began to have an impact on those around her. As you were being born, you began to make a difference in the lives of those around you, and they on those around them.

At first, you were not responsible directly for any of the changes in those lives, or how those people reacted to them. If anyone reacted negatively to your birth, instead of reacting in a godly way, they will have to answer to God for those actions. He will not allow them to blame you on Judgment Day.

As you became old enough to consciously choose between right and wrong, you began to make decisions for which you will be held accountable. If any of those were sins, even if they number in the thousands, God will forgive you if you only ask.

If any of those actions were positive, and by sheer statistics it is probably thousands of such actions, even if they were only smiles, they must have had a positive impact on someone. That means you have already had a tremendous impact on the world!

Each person with whom you have had contact carries with them that memory of you or the impact you made, no matter how small. They make decisions, judgments, and life choices based some-what on your input, good or bad. So how in the world does this give you hope if you have lived a life of which you are already ashamed?

Whether you have lived a life of "shame" or "glory" thus far doesn't keep you from making a tremendous amount of positive difference in the future. Even if you've lived a life of utter crime and evil, if you confess your sins to God and begin to live for Jesus Christ today, the entire rest of your life can make a positive difference in the world.

The Bible tells us that when we are saved, we become new creatures. Our old sin nature is dead, and we are "born again" to live for Christ.

If you begin to serve Christ right where you are, you can make a difference that can change the world forever. How so? Following are several examples:

Think about the greatest evangelist in history. What if that one person wasn't led to Christ by someone else? It is very possible that the leading of the millions to Christ by the evangelist wouldn't have happened, if the one who led that evangelist to the Lord chose not to make a positive difference and be a witness.

What if the last person to be rude to a "crazed gunman" in the news had been nice to him before he became crazed? Maybe one person's kindness would have encouraged the gunman to seek counseling and no one would have died. Have you been rude or insensitive to desperate people who longed for just one smile? Smiles make a difference in the world.

What if just one starving child across the world might have lived until the next shipment of donated food, but someone bought one more soft drink at the movies instead of donating a dollar to the needy? Can anything you do impact the world? Yes, it can!

With Christ, you can make such a great difference in the world, it would probably boggle the most genius of minds! You have been graced by God to learn that today, when many others still have not been given that knowledge.

God does not expect you to impact the whole world at one time, but He has blessed you to live your life for Him one day at a time, starting today! That will make a great difference in the world!

Bible Verses to Overcome Lie #30

- "And of some have compassion, making a difference." Jude 22 (KJV)

- "For so hath the Lord commanded us, saying, I have set thee to be a light of the Gentiles, that thou shouldest be for salvation unto the ends of the earth." Acts 13:47 (KJV)

Related Scripture Passages

- Ephesians 4
- 2 Corinthians 4
- Romans 12
- Matthew 5

Suggested Prayer Focus

1. Pray for forgiveness for any negative differences you have made in the world. Accept that forgiveness with Jesus' love and "press on" with His permission and blessing and for His Honor.

2. Pray every day to see all around you differences you can make, great and small.

3. Pray to recognize that what might seem like a small difference to you can really be a big difference in someone's day, week, or life. You might prevent the "straw that breaks the camel's back" for that person.

4. Pray to recognize that small differences are a part of God's design and will for our lives.

5. Pray to recognize that you will make small differences and great impacts whether you are aware of them or not. Each difference, small or great, will be either to God's glory or Satan's. Be aware and choose for your differences to be for God through Jesus.

6. Pray for any area of life where you would like to make a difference physically but cannot. Praying for others changes the world.

Steps to Take to Overcome Lie #30

1. Commit to making a difference in the world one day at a time, one person at a time, and one small action at a time, without worrying about having a big impact on the whole world. God will take care of your role in such things.

2. Pray everyday for the whole world, for all nations, for specific needs for nations, for individuals, by name or by need, and in specific situations, for God's will to be done. Pray for your enemies.

3. Study your Bible every day. Participate in in-depth Bible studies.

4. Attend church every time it is possible for you. Make it possible to be there often.

5. Tithe.

6. Feed the poor.

7. Clothe the naked.

8. Give water to the thirsty.

9. Visit the sick and afflicted and those in need.

10. Give without expecting anything in return.

11. Tell people about Jesus, how He can save them, and what He has done for you.

12. Help others in times of crisis.

13. Live as a Christian.

14. Speak and conduct yourself as a Christian.

15. Support missionaries with prayer and money.

16. Have no other gods before God.

17. Don't make any graven images.

18. Don't take the Lord's name in vain.

19. Remember the Sabbath and keep it holy.

20. Honor your mother and father.

21. Do not murder.

22. Do not commit adultery.

23. Do not steal.

24. Do not lie.

25. Do not covet.

26. Love God with all your heart and soul and mind. Praise Him.

27. Love your neighbor as yourself.

28. Serve Jesus.

29. Treat others the way you want to be treated.

30. Don't judge others and always be willing to forgive.

NOTES